New technologies
in language learning and teaching

edited by

Ann-Karin Korsvold
Centre for Teacher Education and In-Service Training, Oslo, Norway

Bernd Rüschoff
Pädagogische Hochschule, Karlsruhe, Germany

Education Committee
Council for Cultural Co-operation

Council of Europe Publishing

French edition:

Les nouvelles technologies dans l'apprentissage et l'usage des langues
(à paraître)

ISBN 92-871-3255-0

The opinions expressed in this work are those of the authors and do not necessarily reflect the official policy of the Council for Cultural Co-operation of the Council of Europe.

All correspondence concerning this publication or the reproduction or translation of all or part of the document should be addressed to the Director of Education, Culture and Sport of the Council of Europe (F-67075 Strasbourg Cedex).

The reproduction of extracts is authorised, except for commercial purposes, on condition that the source is quoted.

Council of Europe Publishing
F-67075 Strasbourg Cedex

ISBN 92-871-3254-2
© Council of Europe, 1997
Printed in Germany

TABLE OF CONTENTS

Preface 5

Introduction
Anne-Karin KORSVOLD (Norway) and Bernd RÜSCHOFF (Germany) 7

1   *Computers as cognitive tools in the language classroom*
    Dieter WOLFF (Germany) 17

2   *Lessons from the past, lessons for the future: 20 years of CALL*
    Graham DAVIES (United Kingdom) 27

3   *Old technology, new technology: video makes a come-back*
    Elspeth BROADY (United Kingdom) 53

4   *A pedagogy of the hypermedia*
    Bernard MORO (France) 69

5   *Exploitation of materials in a hypertext environment -*
    gastronomic French
    Aagot ELSLANDE (Norway) 79

6   *Lemmatized concordances of complex utterances:*
    application to language learning
    Mylène GARRIGUES (France) 87

7   *Dealing with information systems. A task-based approach*
    Yvan ROOSELEER (Belgium) 99

8   *Telematics*
    Lis KORNUM (Denmark) 119

9   *Teacher development for the use of information technology*
    Erich ZEHNDER (Germany) 135

Conclusion
Anne-Karin KORSVOLD and Bernd RÜSCHOFF 143

Bibliography 147

Notes on the contributors 155

PREFACE

When launching the Council of Europe Modern Languages Project: *'Language Learning for European Citizenship'* the Education Committee identified a number of educational sectors and themes for priority treatment. In the course of the Project, which was conducted between 1989 and 1996, work in these areas was intensively pursued, partly by studies commissioned from leading experts in the field, but mainly in a series of 'new-style' workshops, attended by colleagues professionally active in the fields concerned. These were nominated by member governments and worked together under the leadership of 'animators' selected by the Council of Europe from among the acknowledged leading experts in Europe.

A 'new-style' workshop was held on the initiative of two co-operating member countries to deal with a theme identified by them as of particular importance. Each 'new-style' workshop had three phases. First, an initiating workshop of some five days' duration was held on the invitation of one member government. Here the aim was to establish the 'state of the art' in the sector or with regard to the theme, to identify areas in which further research and development work was needed, and then to set up an 'action programme' of projects to be carried out by individuals or institutions in two or more member countries under a project co-ordinator. In a second phase, this action programme was then conducted, normally over a two-year period, during which two Progress Reports on the conduct of the Projects were published. In a third phase, the outcomes of the Projects were reported by the Co-ordinators to a follow-up workshop, hosted by the second co-operating member government. Following the discussion of the projects and their products, the workshop concluded by setting out conclusions and recommendations regarding the general development of the field and future policy orientations.

Many of the new-style workshops have dealt with more than one priority sector or theme, and some themes to which a number of governments attached importance were the subjects of a number of workshops. As a result, contributions relating to particular priority sectors and themes were spread over a number of workshop reports, progress reports and independent studies. In addition, constraints on workshop time and report space have placed strict limits on the animators' introductions to workshop themes. The Council of Europe has therefore decided to commission a series of Compendia, each of which would bring together a number of the more significant contributions made to the Project in respect of one of its major areas of concern. In a number of cases this meant leaving aside a number of valuable contributions for which room could not be found in the agreed format, especially since authors have been given the opportunity to develop and up-date their contributions.

The extraordinary, explosive development of the new information and communications technologies in the past decades has undoubtedly been the most powerful factor in the globalisation of modern life, with which our social, economic and political structures are struggling to keep pace. Education is not the least affected, producing an almost intolerable tension between the traditionally encapsulated classroom and an out-of-school environment open to the world - a tension made more acute by the evident need to equip an increasingly aware and critical younger generation to develop a secure sense of identity which is yet flexible and able to respond positively to the challenges of globalisation not only now but in the century to come. New attitudes, knowledge and skills are needed and in acquiring them the new, powerful technological tools which are becoming available have great potential, e.g. in the range and ease of access to large information stores, the immediate availability of cultural products in many languages via satellite, opportunities for real-time exchanges via internet and e-mail, etc.

There are also, of course, great dangers, such as passivity, manipulation, mechanisation, fragmentation, shortening of attention span, etc. It is important that the right lessons are drawn from the disappointments experienced with earlier educational technology, that innovative experimentation with the new technologies should be properly conducted and interaction networks set up using the technologies for the rapid exchange of ideas and experience.

In these respects the new-style workshops conducted in the course of the Project have been successful early steps in a process we hope will now continue under its own momentum. The papers collected here by Anne-Karin Korsvold and Bernd Rüschoff will, we trust, be valuable not only as a successful source of information but as a spur to effective cooperative action.

John L.M. TRIM, Project Director

INTRODUCTION
Anne-Karin KORSVOLD and Bernd RÜSCHOFF

1. The background

Over the past decade the use of computers and new technologies has become an important aspect of foreign language learning. CALL (Computer Assisted Language Learning) and TELL (Technology Enhanced Language Learning) in traditional and innovative applications have enabled the language teaching community to redefine some of the strategies and concepts of teaching and learning. This has been done in terms of enriching classroom activities, reorganising course structures, and providing learners with more autonomous as well as more learner-centred opportunities for learning.

The Council of Europe has been very involved in this process, initially through the workshops of Project No. 12 "Learning and teaching modern languages for communication." As early as 1983 it was suggested, at the opening symposium of that project in Delphi, that the use of new technological devices in language teaching for communication, as well as ways of working within multi-media systems, should be amongst the themes to be given special consideration at the series of workshops proposed for Project 12. (see. Trim, 1988, pp. 31-33) In addition, it was anticipated that participants of Project 12 workshops would deal with the development of learner autonomy and learner-centred approaches including the integration of new technologies into language learning applications. As a result, a number of workshops in Project 12 explored new technologies and CALL (Computer Assisted Language Learning), and some of the key specialists in this field contributed to these workshops. It must be pointed out that quite a number of the findings and recommendations of this series of workshops have helped to shape current positions on language learning methodology and the exploitation of IT (Information Technology) resources in foreign language learning.

More recently, two of the "new-style" international workshops held in the context of the Council for Cultural Co-operation (CDCC) Modern Languages Project "Language Learning for European Citizenship" (1989-1997) continued the debate. These were Workshops 7A/B on "Using information and communication technologies in modern language teaching and learning in Europe" and Workshops 9A/B on "The use of new technologies in the learning and teaching of modern languages in vocationally oriented education [upper secondary (16-19) and adult education]." The overall aims of these workshops were defined as follows: telecommunications and multimedia technologies should be embedded in a principled and harmonious approach to language teaching; the design of multimedia applications specifically for language learning should be based on sound pedagogical and methodological principles such as the promotion of learner autonomy and "learning to learn" rather than purely technological considerations.

Based on the findings of these workshops, this compendium presents an overview of the potential of Information Technology and CALL in the context of language learning with particular emphasis on resource exploitation. Contributors to this compendium, who have participated in Workshops 7 and 9, were invited to address the necessary theoretical considerations and to present case studies, examples of good practice and updated results of their project work. The first two contributions are intended as survey articles, with Dieter Wolff discussing the theoretical framework and Graham Davies presenting a state-of-the art overview of the development of language teaching and learning technology. The following papers then present work done before, during and after the workshops in Research and Development Projects. In the course of this introduction the editors offer their own views on the theme and refer the reader to the relevant paper.

2. Theoretical framework - overview of software

One of the key questions underlying all the discussions and projects at the Council of Europe workshops on the use of new technologies in language learning, concerned the pedagogical and methodological principles which would ensure that multimedia technologies are firmly embedded in a principled and harmonious approach to language teaching. It became evident that linguists and teachers have begun to reappraise some earlier interpretations of a communicative approach to language learning. Current "post-communicative" trends in this field are based on the results of Second Language Acquisition research and on the findings of cognitive psychology. However, it must be noted that these trends do not indicate a return to traditional concepts of drill and practice. Quite the contrary, as rather than the traditional instructivist paradigm of learning in a purely tutorial mode, a cognitive-constructivist paradigm is seen as an important methodological basis for real innovation in foreign language learning.

A methodology based on such principles focuses, among other things, on "learner orientation, process orientation and learner autonomy." (Wolff, 1994, p. 407). Language learning should be regarded as a process of information gathering and knowledge processing. In such a process the interaction between previously acquired knowledge and the new information leads to the acquisition of new knowledge. Consequently, language learning is seen as an interactive, dynamic process, in which new knowledge is often acquired when learners are placed in a situation where they can explore and discover language by means of utilising sources and resources, rather than in a context of formal instruction. In such a scenario, learners combine new information with previous factual (declarative) and procedural (strategic) knowledge and draw new conclusions from this process. (see Rüschoff, 1992) By means of problem-solving tasks, hypothesis formation and hypothesis validation, both the content of learning materials and the learning process itself become more transparent and perceivable. Holec, for example, has pointed out in his Council of Europe study on autonomy and self-directed learning that both knowledge in the field of language competence, i.e. language awareness, and knowledge in the field of language learning, i.e. learning processes and learning behaviour, need to be developed in language learning. (see Holec, 1996, p. 10) This position seems to favour a constructivist approach, which emphasises task-based learning.

8

As a result, a tools enhanced approach to the exploitation of IT, where learners work as much as possible with authentic and semi-authentic materials in the context of authentic, real-world-based tasks, must be regarded as the most promising approach to the integration of new technologies into the language curriculum. The effectiveness of traditional computer assisted tutorials and CALL teachware should be regarded with more scepticism than in the past. However, technology enhanced language learning, in the form of using IT tools to assist learning processes, must be regarded as part of the innovative potential of new technologies. Therefore, it is claimed that apart from the development of multi-media learning packages, the use of technological tools of the real world, such as word processing and data processing, as well as electronic publications and so-called cognitive tools, will contribute significantly to a successful integration of these tools into more effective curricula for language learning.

The issues outlined above, and the implications for the use of new technology in language learning, are addressed by Dieter Wolff (one of the keynote speakers at Workshop 9B) who explores the potential role of computers as cognitive tools in the language classroom. His paper provides a detailed insight into current methodological reflections and the principles of language learning within a cognitive-constructivist framework.

In the light of what has been suggested so far, it could be argued that IT resources should only be used in the form of authentic electronically published materials and cognitive tools. (see Wolff, 1994) After all, "effective tools are those that support cognitive processes ... or allow learners to generate and test hypotheses in meaningful problem-solving tasks." (Jonassen, 1992, p.6) Nevertheless, it can be argued that a broader view is needed and that both positive adaptations of traditional tutorial software and the exploitation of innovative tools need to be considered when discussing IT and TELL resources for language learning. In the second survey article, Graham Davies, one of the pioneers in this field, presents an overview of developments in language learning and teaching technology during the last twenty years. This paper not only describes and discusses various examples of old and new software, but also contains a host of references as to where and how to find further information on the subject and how to join networks for future co-operation in the field of CALL & TELL.

As not all readers have access to the latest state-of-the-art multimedia technology, the editors take this opportunity to refer to the vast number of programs available which translate traditional paper-based exercise formats into CALL and TELL software. These programs should be judged in terms of the kind of flexibility they offer and the types of interactivity integrated into their exercise formats. Flexible software of this type integrates help files and additional references into tutorial or exploratory interaction. For example, learners working on an exercise dealing with technical terminology can be encouraged to consult references from technical manuals and other semi-authentic materials included in the help files, producing a learning situation where they can deduct or construct the appropriate meaning and semantic and syntactic functionality of such terms. This could be regarded a first step towards developing the kind of learning strategies mentioned above and thus contribute to the success of using other kinds of (cognitive) tools later on in the curriculum. This kind of learning will actually lead to some form of language awareness rather than simple structural knowledge that usually results from simple and repetitive drill and practice exercises.

In relation to the use of such traditional software concepts, the availability and value of many of these materials as authoring tools should not be underestimated. In contrast to dedicated software, authoring tools provide teachers with the option of creating their own exercises and language games without the need to program or any in-depth knowledge of computing. Such tools also help teachers to appreciate how easy the use of CALL and TELL in their language classes can be. In addition, authoring tools of this kind should be used more often in the context of learning projects, where learners are encouraged to organise language structures or vocabulary into exercise templates or databases. In this way, they do not simply practice vocabulary and grammar. On the contrary, such tasks are intended to develop language awareness and can actually be regarded as an initial form of project-based learning. CALL authorware used in such a role, as templates for knowledge organisation, could be described as a first example of the cognitive tools to be discussed later.

3. Case studies and Research and Development Projects

Technology old and new

It can be argued that the most effective way of benefiting from new technologies, for the purpose of innovation in language learning, would be an integrated exploitation of both traditional learnware with exploratory elements and newly developed tools and resources. However, when discussing recent developments in multimedia applications, one must not forget video technology and its potential contribution to new ways of learning. At Workshop 9, one of the R & D Project groups looked at this particular problem, and their results are documented in Elspeth Broady's article on the re-emergence of video technology. In addition, this contribution discusses important issues concerning the use of interactive video as opposed to CD-ROM-based multimedia applications. Video is discussed as a creative medium in the context of a task-based framework and relevant examples are presented

Multimedia and hypertext technology

A number of dedicated exercises and courseware with integrated multimedia options have been published, recently culminating in packages with some form of voice processing and speech recognition. (see Graham Davies's survey article) Such tools are also available as authoring packages, both in the format of pre-defined exercise templates with exploratory elements or in the form of hypertext compilers. In general, where information gathering and processes of knowledge perception and knowledge construction are involved, any kind of HYPERTEXT application and hypermedia will fit into this category of learning, by providing learners and teachers with the appropriate utilities. Such tools enable them to put together electronic books with hyperlinks into multimedia and other references. Most "programming" operations are based on standard word processing skills, so that even less experienced teachers and learners can use the package to integrate text, video clips, sound files, animations, graphics and pictures into flexible hypertexts. Footnotes and external exercises can also be added to such materials. Multimedia hypertext authoring tools fit well into a theoretical framework of cognitive-constructivist learning, particularly if learners are encouraged to use such systems as tools to put together their own electronic multimedia and hypertext dossiers in the context of learning projects.

At "new-style" Workshop 9B, a number of project groups dealt with hypertext applications. Their case studies are represented by Bernard Moro's and Aagot Elslande's papers. Bernard Moro's contribution, in particular, exemplifies that in cognitive terms, the assets of hypermedia, as opposed to other documentary systems, firstly lie in their navigational mode, which is direct and random rather than sequential. They also lie in the fact that abstractions can be made concrete and visualised by easy access to pictures. Thus metaphors may be displayed on screen, mental processes such as unconscious grammatical transformations can be translated into animations that are crystal-clear to the learner. Thus cultural data may be injected, in sound or visual form, within a perfectly user-friendly environment. Such applications are content-oriented, i.e., they presented a document within a didactic environment whose major purpose was to enhance understanding and help learners access the meaning of a text which per se was the centre of the software proposed. In addition, however, the hypermedia application would become an environment devoted to acquiring strategies whose various aspects the learner would absorb, whose validity he would assess in the in vitro shelter of the computer, before putting them to the in vivo test of reality when confronting any document of comparable sort. This would be, in educational terms, a flight simulator of sorts, one where the learner / flyer would test his skills before using them solo, in real flight, i.e in real world language use and language processing.

It is important when designing hypertext and multi-media applications to consider carefully how information and help can be presented to the learner via the computer keyboard. Above all, help must promote strategy building and be cognition and knowledge construction oriented, rather than just geared towards task solving. In the light of what has been said about the importance of cognitive processes and strategies in language learning and acquisition, we agree with Pressley & Associates, who propose that, "strategies should not be taught as a separate topic in the curriculum. Rather, they should be taught throughout the curriculum as part of the actual academic tasks that students encounter." (Pressley & Ass., 1990, p. 16). This statement is relevant to the educational design of IT resources in as much as it should be the basic guideline for curricula development. Such considerations must also be kept in mind when discussing dedicated multimedia and CD-ROM based resources. In recent years a number of dedicated CD-ROM courses have been published, which draw on the ideas and concepts of hypermedia. Unfortunately, quite a number of these still follow the pattern of traditional exercises embedded into a multimedia learning environment.

CD-ROM resources, databases and information systems

Apart from the kind of hypertext authoring packages mentioned above, an increasing number of databases on CD-ROM are also available. The editors feel that the most effective contribution IT will make to an innovative development in language learning methodology could come from the exploitation of electronic publications and CD-ROM resources (such as text databases and encyclopaedia) both in course preparation and as part of learning projects. Obviously, teachers can exploit such resources for their coursework by, for example, extracting texts and animations relating to a given subject from an encyclopaedia and adapting them for classroom use. Recently, major educational publishers have published tools which provide assistance for teachers when exploiting such texts from authentic sources for use as classroom material. These tools check texts against a curriculum-based database in order to facilitate editing and adaptation for use with less advanced learners; some even integrate a number of macros for the generation of exercises.

Ways of dealing with such information systems on the basis of a task based approach are discussed by Yvan Rooseleer. His work reflects activities which were part of both Workshop 7 and 9, but focuses on languages for special purposes applications. It is argued that the world described in a database system will provide learners and teachers with a realistic context in which a task can be situated. In view of the theoretical concepts discussed in this paper, the editors feel that the exploitation of such resources as part of project-based learning might be a rather fruitful approach. Again, learners should be encouraged to put together multimedia presentations, using existing presentation and authoring tools, on the basis of their own research in text corpora or encyclopaedia. Such scenarios for language learning come very close to introducing forms of cognitive-constructivist learning into the language classroom.

Cognitive tools and concordancing

Cognitive tools illustrate yet another form of the exploitation of IT in foreign language learning. As Dieter Wolff stated in his contribution to Workshop 9B, examples of such tools include *semantic networking*, where the computer helps the learner to understand the storage and interrelations of concepts in the human brain, and *expert systems* with computers helping the learner to restructure knowledge and thus learn to make better use of this learning facility. Another example would be the simulation of complex scenarios which contribute to an understanding of the importance of different parameters in a complex problem solving processes. Other cognitive tools include software templates which help learners to organise their knowledge, and data-processing tools as such tools enable learners to understand the complexity and functionality of structures and vocabulary and help to develop their knowledge perception and knowledge processing abilities.

Hypertexts and authoring templates, such as vocabulary databases have already been mentioned. However, the editors consider that concordancing programs are probably the most widely usable information processing-based cognitive tools in language learning. These tools represent a special kind of application, as their exploitation does not necessarily require the use of computers with the learners themselves. A number of feasible scenarios have been described in detail in a book on the subject of concordancers in language learning by Chris Tribble included in the references listed below. (see Tribble & Jones, 1989) Further examples are discussed in Mylene Garrigue's contribution dealing with the use of lemmatized concordances of complex utterances in language learning.

Basically, concordancers can be seen as tools that allow for "researching the company that words keep" (Johns, 1986) and thus for developing language awareness. Concordancers provide access to any electronic text, i.e. a text available on the computer or from a CD-ROM based corpus or database and search for the occurrence of particular words or structures, or combinations of words (e.g. verbs and prepositions). These are then listed in one-line contexts and these lists can be used as the basis for discussions about word-formation, language structure, and (meaning of) vocabulary. Thus learners discover for themselves the rules for using a particular structure or word. In addition to exploiting texts with concordancing tools for discovery-based learning projects and process-oriented forms of learning, computer assisted exercises can be generated on the basis of searches with a concordancer using authoring tools, such as Tim John's CONTEXT.

The editors feel that this particular use of computer technology in language learning concurs with the argument stated above that learners should be provided with an opportunity to develop strategies on which they can build once the language class is finished. What is important is the fact that concordancers can be used with any textual source. Therefore, it opens language classes to the use and integration of up-to-date and often authentic language even at lower levels. All the CD-ROM based text corpora and databases mentioned above can be used to search for suitable texts and subsequently form the basis for applications of the kind described here, thus greatly enriching the scope and content of classroom activities.

Telecommunications

Finally, we need to address the issue of telecommunications and its growing importance in language learning. Quite a number of the tools and resources described in this paper have now in part been transferred onto a globally accessible platform via the INTERNET and the World Wide Web. New editions of CD-ROM resources and encyclopaedia even offer the option of accessing regular updates from the INTERNET to add to the information available locally. In recent months a number of suggestions have been made as to the exploitation of these means of globally exchanging and accessing information. One of the obvious options for (language) learning is, of course, to tap into the "libraries of the world" by means of telecommunications. Lis Kornum's paper deals with various aspects of exploiting telematics for language learning purposes.

Apart from using telematics as a means for tapping into global resources and information systems, telecommunications needs to be regarded in terms of integrating such communication and interaction channels into teleco-operative and telecommunicative learning projects. It is with such scenarios that a communicative learning situation achieves almost real world authenticity. Real-life communication in learning projects on the web and cooperation with real project partners, possibly native speakers of the target language, is much more in line with innovative approaches to language learning than traditional communicative learning scenarios in the context of simulated communication in isolated classrooms.

This was confirmed by the project groups at Workshop 9B dealing with telematics. This group reported that in their project work communication by e-mail meant an increase of personal contact alongside the electronic contact. Communication by e-mail was experienced as personal, live and real, something quite different from sending a fax or a letter. The main difference was the amount of communication by e-mail leading to an increase of personal contact alongside the electronic interactivity involved in the communication process. In addition, aspects of intercultural learning and related competences much needed in an increasingly globalised working environment can be experienced while learning the foreign language.

Lastly, telecommunication can be used in the context of teleco-operative tutoring and distance learning. Here, new and more direct and interactive channels of communication can be made available to ensure a closer and more fruitful co-operation between the learning partners in a virtual (distance learning) classroom. In our opinion, such applications are of tremendous importance for language learning, as they allow for more flexible use of the limited time sometimes available for language learning. In addition, telecommunication could be used to set up on-going learning forums and continuous language training for professionals, thus extending language learning options beyond the sometimes limited scope of formal classes and curricula.

Teacher development

Although most of the practical IT applications for language learning are based on software and tools which are fairly user-friendly, teacher training is also an important subject for this compendium. There are various reasons for this. The new communication and information technologies are both complex and expensive. Hard- and software development are sometimes moving so quickly that the average language teacher often sees more difficulties than advantages when attempting to make effective use of these new tools in language learning. However, the ability to make use of IT tools and resources will be one of the basic skills future teachers will have to acquire as part of their training. Consequently, basic skills in handling authoring software and hypertext templates as well as the ability to work with databases and exploit electronic publications and encyclopaedia needs to be trained. However, it seems to be of even greater significance to make teachers aware of the innovative potential of such resources and familiarise them with the appropriate pedagogical and methodological principles for their exploitation.

As a result of such considerations, the issue of teacher training and new technology was discussed intensively in the course of the new-style workshops. Apart from the need for a technology related component in initial training, various aspects of in-service training were researched and tested by one of the R & D project groups at Workshop 9. In this compendium, Erich Zehnder's paper briefly summarises the topic, while further information can be obtained from a brochure and an accompanying video produced by the group, which document the results and the various pilot seminars conducted as part of the project.

4. Preliminary conclusion

It is hoped that the selection of topics presented in this compendium reflects the essence of the deliberations in this introduction. The case studies and examples of good practice selected are intended to throw light on the various considerations concerning IT in the foreign language classroom. Furthermore, they are in themselves illustrations of the development that has taken place within the world of CALL and TELL during the years the Research and Development groups were at work. The period from 1991 (Workshop 7A in Sèvres) until 1995 (Workshop 9B in Karlsruhe) were exciting and innovative years in both language learning and IT methodology, and it is hoped that the excitement is reflected in this volume.

References

Reports on Council of Europe international workshops related to the theme:
(available in the language indicated by the title; 7B is a combination of English and French).

Rapport de l'Atelier 7A. *Moyens technologiques de l'information et de la communication au service de l'enseignement/apprentissage des langues vivantes en Europe.* Sèvres (France) décembre 1991. Doc. CC-LANG (92) Atelier 7A. Coordonné par M. Garrigues.

Report on Workshop 7B/Rapport de l'Atelier 7B. *Using information and communication technologies in modern language teaching and learning in Europe/Moyens technologiques de l'information et de la communication au service de l'enseignement/apprentissage des langues vivantes en Europe.* Gillelje (Denmark/Danemark) April/avril 1994. Doc. CC-LANG (95) Workshop 7B/Atelier 7A. Compiled and edited by/coordonné par L. Kornum.

Report on Workshop 9A.. *The use of new technologies in the learning and teaching of modern languages in vocationally oriented education [upper secondary (16-19) and adult education].* Grimstad (Norway), September 1992. Doc. CC-LANG (92) Workshop 9A. Compiled and edited by A.-K. Korsvold.

Report on Workshop 9B. *The use of new technologies in the learning and teaching of modern languages in vocationally oriented education [upper secondary (16-19) and adult education].* Karlsruhe (Germany), April 1995. Doc. CC-LANG (95) Workshop 9B. Compiled and edited by B. Rüschoff.

Available free of charge from: Modern Languages Section
Council of Europe
F-67075 Strasbourg Cedex

Other publications:

Benjamin, R.I. & Blunt, J. (1992): "Critical IT Issues: The Next Ten Years". In: *Sloan Management Review*, MIT, Summer 1992, pp. 7-19.

Jackson, M.J. (1988): "Siren Shapes: Exploratory and Constructive Hypertexts". In: *Academic Computing*, November, pp. 10-42.

Johns, T. (1986): "Micro-Concord". In: *Triangle 5*: pp. 120-134.

Jonassen, D. (1992): "Evaluating constructivistic learning". In: Duffy, T.M. & Jonassen, D. H. (eds.): *Constructivism and the Technology of Instruction: A Conversation*. Hillsdale, N.J.: Erlbaum 1992, pp. 137-148.

Jones/Fortescue (1989): *Using Computers in the Language Classroom*. Harlow: Longman.

Jung, Udo O.H. (1993): *International Bibliography of Computer Assisted Language Learning, vol II*. Frankfurt: Lang.

Moro, B. (1996): "Hypermedia software applications: from content oriented to methodology oriented design". In Report for Workshop 9B.

Pelfrêne, A. (1986): "Lecticiel". In: *Triangle 6*, pp. 135-142.

Pressley, M. & Ass. (1990): *Cognitive Strategy Instruction that really Improves Childrens' Academic Performance*. Cambridge, MA, Brookline Books.

ReCALL Software Guide No. 3 (1993). University of Hull, CTI Centre for Modern Languages.

Rüschoff, B. & Wolff, D. (1991): "Developing and using interactive audio for foreign language learning". In: *CALL AUSTRIA 15*, pp. 186-203.

Rüschoff, B. (1993): "Language Learning and Information Technology: state of the art". In: *CALICO Journal 10 (3)*, pp. 5-17.

Tribble, C. & Jones, G. (1990): *Concordances in Classroom*. Harlow: Longman.

Trim, J.L.M. (1988). *Council of Europe Project No. 12 "Learning and teaching modern languages for communication" - Consolidated report on the programme of international workshops for trainers of teachers of modern languages 1984-87*. Strasbourg: Council of Europe.

Wendt, M. (1996): *Konstruktivistische Fremdsprachendidaktik: Lerner- und handlungsorientierter Fremdsprachenunterricht aus neuer Sicht*. Tübingen: Gunter Narr Verlag.

Wolff, D. (1994a): "Neue methodische Ansätze im Fremdsprachenunterricht: Ein Überblick". In: Kohn, J. & Wolff, D. (eds.): *New Methodologies in Foreign Language Learning and Teaching*. Szombathely: Berzsenyi College, pp. 8-24.

Wolff, D. (1994b): "Der Konstruktivismus: Ein neues Paradigma in der Fremdsprachendidaktik?" In: *Die Neueren Sprachen 93 (5)*, pp. 407-429.

1. COMPUTERS AS COGNITIVE TOOLS IN THE LANGUAGE CLASSROOM

Dieter WOLFF - Germany

Introduction

All over the world there are discussions going on about how to use computers adequately in the foreign language classroom. Opinions can be represented on a kind of continuum. At the one end, there are practical language teachers, but also a number of theoreticians, who advocate an approach which favours the tutorial functions of the computer, those who would like to use it to generate formal exercises and activities; they usually stress the computer's ability to control and correct learner input in such exercises. At the other end, there are teachers who dislike, on principle, the idea of making computers available for language learning. They claim that it is not worth spending valuable time reflecting upon a technology which has no function in the context of communicative language teaching, since this emphasises human communication and not interaction with a machine. Needless to say, neither one nor the other position is tenable any longer.

In my contribution I will discuss an approach which is located somewhere in the middle of the continuum. The computer has become the most important and the most flexible tool in the working world but we have not yet managed to successfully integrate all its functions into the language classroom. The idea of using the computer as a tool in learning is not new, among others I put it forward myself. (see Wolff 1994a) Here I would like to develop this idea further.

Until recently, the tool functions of the computer were defined as those functions which we use in our everyday activities, for example data storage and sorting, word processing, data transfer in telecommunications applications etc. But now another term has arisen and is being discussed more and more extensively in the general context of learning theories, and this is the term "cognitive tool". In my paper I will look at the computer as a cognitive tool, that is to say as a tool which can help the human learner to use his/her cognition more effectively. This does not mean that the computer itself possesses inherent cognitive abilities, it simply means that it can do things which can aid the learner in his/her information processing and learning.

In my paper I will first discuss, very briefly, my ideas on learning which are strongly influenced by cognitive psychology and constructivist theories. In the second part, I will talk about the computer as a cognitive tool in knowledge construction. In the third part, I will go into rather more detail about the possibilities of using the computer as a cognitive learning tool in the foreign language classroom.

17

Learning as knowledge construction

The idea of learning as knowledge construction is the basis of the theoretical framework of my assumptions on language learning and the use of the computer in the language classroom. Learning as knowledge construction is a formula which has become a kind of *leitmotiv* both in cognitive psychology and in constructivism.

One of the central assumptions of cognitive psychology is that the human information processor makes use of a large repertoire of processing strategies and other mental operations in order to process information and to optimise the processing system, i.e. to control the acquisition of new knowledge, the reorganisation of and access to the knowledge store. The whole complex activity is called "learning" in cognitive psychology.

Constructivists postulate that there is no reality independent of the human being. Reality is always constructed by the human being and exists, therefore, only subjectively in his or her brain. In personal construct theory as developed by Kelly (1963), it is claimed that every human being has developed a personal theory of the world which is continuously being tested and revised. As in cognitive psychology, learning is seen by constructivists as an independent construction process which is based on individual learner knowledge and therefore leads to different learning results for each learner. There are no learning processes which go beyond the subjective construction of meaning and the assimilation of the results of such construction processes with the knowledge already acquired. Learning necessitates the use of specific strategies in order to control the construction process. Learning also implies the restructuring of already acquired knowledge and is always embedded in social contexts; the interaction with others is of great importance. Learning is a process of self-organisation by the learner and can only be organised if the learner takes the full responsibility for his own learning.

Constructivists have developed a number of specific learning principles which are of interest in the context of foreign language learning. I will just mention four (see also Wolff 1994b):

1. Learning in general, and language learning in particular must be embedded in an authentic and complex learning environment. Only within a rich learning environment can the learner adequately use his personal constructs and thus test and verify his hypotheses about a learning item.

2. It is not only the learning environments that should be rich and complex; the learning content itself should be represented in all its complexity. A reduction of content, a systematisation of learning items and too rigid grading is detrimental to the learning process.

3. Only abilities and knowledge which can be used in everyday reality should be focused upon in the classroom. This principle is related to one of the key concepts of constructivism, i.e. that the learner must be made responsible for his own learning. A learner can only feel responsible when he is made to recognise the importance of what he is learning for his own life ("getting the learner involved").

4.   The construction of knowledge as a process for which the learner is responsible must be undertaken autonomously; learning is not a process of instruction but rather of construction (see also Mercer 1995). A learner must learn how to adequately use his/her knowledge in the learning process, he must learn to restructure his knowledge base after each learning process and he must learn to automatise his knowledge so that he can access it at any time. If learning is such an autonomous, creative construction process, then it can only be influenced by providing help for the learner in his knowledge construction process. Help can be provided in different ways, for example by making the learner acquainted with learning strategies or with learning tools. Learning how to learn is the key issue and learning tools are very helpful in this context.

The computer as a cognitive tool in knowledge construction

A tentative definition of the term 'cognitive tool'

Let me begin with Jonassen's (1992) definition of a cognitive tool:

> Effective cognitive tools are those that support cognitive processes, those that enable learners to engage in higher order thinking, that help learners engage in cognitive processes that would normally be impossible, or that allow learners to generate and test hypotheses in meaningful problem-solving situations (Jonassen 1992:6).

Sharples (1988) looks at the functions of cognitive tools in a slightly different way. He is of the opinion that it is possible, with the help of cognitive tools, to externalise human cognition, to make it transparent for the learner and thus to improve his learning processes. Seen from this perspective cognitive tools have a consciousness-raising function, the learner is made conscious of his own learning and will better understand the different ways to solve a learning task.

To sum up, there are two major functions which cognitive tools can fulfil in the learning process:

1.   They help learners to improve their own abstraction and generalisation processes, to construct and test hypotheses and to solve learning problems.

2.   They represent, in an operationalised and transparent form, strategies of knowledge construction and thus they externalise human cognition.

The computer as a cognitive tool

A number of theoreticians who have discussed the possibilities of using computers in learning assume that the true strength of this technology in a pedagogical context lies in the possibilities it offers as a cognitive tool. Computers, they argue, are more flexible than all the other teaching and learning aids; they are dynamic and can represent processes as processes and make them really transparent.

In a volume on cognitive tools which was published in 1992, Kommers describes a number of highly complex technology-enhanced cognitive tools which can assist the construction of knowledge and make learning more transparent. Although not all of these tools are suitable for the foreign language classroom, I would like to mention a few of them here to make the idea of the computer as a cognitive tool clearer:

a. *Templates*: A template as a cognitive tool provides help for the learner in his knowledge organisation. Classification of knowledge into the categories provided, sorting these categories and testing category matching is a first step in knowledge structuring and makes knowledge ready for integration into the knowledge store.

b. *Expert systems*: They should not be seen in this context as ready-made systems developed by system engineers but as databases which the learner himself builds up during the knowledge construction process. The computer program simply serves to store the knowledge intelligently. In using such a tool, learning is promoted because the learner has to structure the newly acquired knowledge in order to fit it into the system.

c. *Hypertext-systems and other databases*: These are ready-made flexible knowledge systems which should be used actively by the learner in order to extend his own knowledge. Hypertext-systems have one advantage compared with conventional databases: they not only provide knowledge immediately, they also model the choices the learner makes to acquire the knowledge needed, and this makes it possible afterwards to reconstruct the ways in which a specific piece of knowledge was obtained.

d. *Simulations*: The simulation of complex scenarios makes it easier for the learner to understand the importance of different parameters in a complex problem-solving process. The possibility of varying the parameters in a simulation contributes to the development of the learner's problem-solving abilities.

It should have become clear that, in general, knowledge construction processes can be developed in at least in two different ways by using computers as cognitive tools:

1. Knowledge construction processes can be made transparent so that the learner is conscious of them, and

2. computers can provide classificatory systems which simplify knowledge processing.

The computer as a learning tool in the foreign language classroom

The importance of the computer as a learning tool in the foreign language classroom has been emphasised repeatedly in recent publications. A distinction has been made between four types of tool functions: the text processing function, the database function, the data manipulating function (concordance programs) and the data transfer function (telecommunications). Taking into account the results of modern learning psychology as sketched out in the first part of my paper, the question of whether these tools are really valid in the foreign language classroom can be looked at from another perspective. We can ask whether these tools also possess features which make them valuable cognitive tools for the language classroom or whether it is necessary to develop other tools which can better fulfil this cognitive function.

I believe that the learning tools mentioned above do have an inherent cognitive potential. We can distinguish between at least three cognitive functions:

1. Computers make the complexity of learning items more transparent. I will look at electronic dictionaries (database function).

2. Computers make the complexity of the language to be learnt more transparent. I will look at concordance programs as cognitive tools.

3. Computers can help learners to master complex linguistic tasks. I will look at word processing and its possible extensions.

Computers make the complexity of learning items more transparent

I would like to discuss, in this context, two learning tools which could become cognitive tools in the true sense of the term if a number of their present characteristics were improved, namely learner dictionaries (with an authoring function) and electronic dictionaries on CD-ROM.

On the software market there are a few electronic learner dictionaries which are organised as templates and which make it possible for learners to build up their own personal dictionaries. From the point of view of software design, these templates are comparable to the templates whose potential for cognitive learning in general I mentioned a moment ago. Such dictionaries have the advantage that words and their meanings can be found very easily and that the learner can put together the vocabulary according to different criteria (morphological, syntactic, semantic etc.). Commercially available dictionaries, however, have one serious disadvantage - they do not offer enough different fields to store the necessary information. Usually there are fields provided for the word form, the definition, examples, register, meaning in the source language. Such dictionaries would be much more helpful in the learning process if the number of fields could be increased. Context, semantic field, grammatical code, synonym/antonym relations are also important information for the learner in order to build up a semantic network.

In vocabulary work, such templates have a classifying function. Learners collect information about the word to be inserted in the dictionary from all kinds of sources, from the textbook, from dictionaries, from authentic sources etc. The prestructuring function of such a template makes learners process information in an orderly way and helps them to integrate vocabulary into their mental lexicon. Working with such templates, then, leads to more intensive knowledge structuring and thus to more adequate processing with respect to the integration of the words into the mental lexicon.

Electronic dictionaries and large-scale encyclopaedias have become more and more numerous since CD-ROM technology made it possible to handle large amounts of data. To my knowledge, the first CD-ROM dictionary was the *Oxford English Dictionary* which was published three years ago in a WINDOWS version; others are *Collins Cobuild* and in Germany the *Duden Dictionary*. Bilingual dictionaries are less common and not yet in a presentable form. Encyclopaedias are very common, on the other hand, the *Encarta*, the *American Encyclopaedia* and *Bertelsmann Encyclopaedia* should be mentioned.

All electronic dictionaries are, of course, of interest for the language classroom. At the touch of a button they offer information about the meaning of a word and they usually provide a large number of examples. Unfortunately many of these dictionaries are, however, only electronic copies of existing book versions. This is very common, especially with German products, and the technological potential the computer has is hardly ever exhausted. It is very difficult, for example, to sort the vocabulary according to specific criteria (an exception here is the OED, where sorting is, however, a fairly tricky affair as well). In most dictionaries it is not possible to directly pass over to a reference by clicking onto the word which refers to the other entry. The Oxford English Dictionary provides two help functions which facilitate cognitive processing; a mind map which represents the structure of an entry, and a facility to reconstruct the way in which the search process was undertaken.

These latter options indicate what help functions these dictionaries could be equipped with in order to facilitate dictionary work. A dictionary which provides such help functions - which helps to organise vocabulary according to formal, semantic and functional criteria, which makes it possible to bring together entries of synonyms and antonyms or other related words, and which models search processes - would be a cognitive tool in the sense of the definition given above and would substantially facilitate vocabulary learning. Similar recommendations could be given for encyclopaedias. They use the multimedia potential of the CD-ROM extensively, but they do not usually provide all the processing and learning help which is technically possible.

Computers make the complexity of the language to be learnt more transparent

In a modern concept of language learning which emphasises learner autonomy and which regards knowledge construction as an independent process, learners must be provided with tools which make the complexity of the language the learner encounters more transparent. In the context of my paper, concordance programs, which I include in the data manipulation function of the computer, can be attributed a cognitive tool function.

Concordance programs make it possible to search for recurrent patterns in electronic texts and to present them on the screen together with their contexts. Concordance programs can present the vocabulary of a corpus in alphabetical order and in an order of decreasing frequency. In principle, such programs function according to a simple pattern-search procedure; they are rudimentary and old-fashioned from the point of view of modern computer technology. From the perspective of cognitive learning psychology, however, a concordance program is a very powerful cognitive tool which makes learners recognise linguistic regularities better, formulate hypotheses about linguistic data and test their hypotheses about these data. This tool makes the complexity of specific aspects of the language to be learnt more transparent and can thus be of help in order to discover the rule system of the new language.

In a number of smaller research projects on the use of concordance programs in the classroom (Eck/Legenhausen/Wolff 1994), we were able to observe the potential of this tool in the learning process. It was surprising how many different hypotheses about language learners formulated and tested on the basis of the text corpora at their disposal. They looked into grammatical structures, they studied coherence features and collocations. In literary texts they enquired how authors characterise their protagonists, in letters they analysed forms of address and letter ending formulas. Working with a concordance was motivating for the learners; according to them it contributed to increasing their knowledge about the new language and to understanding its grammar better.

In the context of a LINGUA project we are trying together with a number of other European universities to develop a concordance program which can access words and also more complex structures in the original language and in translations into other European languages. I believe that it is, in particular, the principle of contrastivity inherent in our approach which will make this parallel concordancing program a valuable tool to stimulate learners' cognition.

I think it has become clear why I would like to classify concordance programs as cognitive tools. The computer makes the complexity of the language to be learnt more transparent, and it helps the learner to gain insights into the language to be learnt which are not based on strange linguistic categories and rules but which he has discovered himself. Language awareness is developed in this way; grammar teaching is replaced by discovery learning. The concordance program as a cognitive tool provides categories to classify the complexity of linguistic data; it stimulates the learner's cognition and thus improves his knowledge-construction processes.

Computers can help learners to master complex linguistic tasks

I will now take a look at the ways in which computers can be of help in mastering more complex linguistic tasks. I have chosen writing as probably the most complex linguistic activity and word processing as the most popular tool function of the computer. As is generally known, computer technology has developed very powerful instruments to master the writing process, instruments which show a number of features which make it possible to include them among the cognitive tools. Everybody knows that a word processing system consists of a number of modules, the word processing system per se and a number of help functions, spelling checkers, thesauri, grammar checkers etc.

There is practically no research on the use of the help function of the word processor. In our own research we found that our students hardly use what is offered. This has something to do with the fact that thesauri are not yet very user-friendly and not very helpful. The large number of other extensions (note pads, think sheets) are not very popular either.

In our research on the use of the word processor in second language writing, however, it also became clear that neither the word processor nor its extensions can sufficiently support the higher order processes which are necessary to write a complex text. Writing research has recently stressed the point that writing a text - whether in one's first or second language - not only necessitates lexical and grammatical knowledge but also a repertoire of strategic knowledge in order to adapt the text to be written to a specific reader, a specific aim and a specific text format. Writing a text in a foreign language also requires additional knowledge on the writing conventions of the other language and culture.

It also emerged from our writing research that it is the culture-specific text formats which cause particular difficulty in second language writing. By text formats I do not mean simply text types but also the local text structures within a text type which can be very different in different cultures. An example will make clear what I mean: the text type "business letter" not only exhibits differences in its global structure in German and English, but its local structures, for example the beginning or the end of the letter, are different too. Such differences are not only differences in the way certain formulae are used, they also relate to the internal structure of a text paragraph, to the presentation of information, quite often even to putting in or leaving out information.

In order to help learners with such higher order writing tasks we are in the process of developing, in the context of another LINGUA project, a cognitive writing tool which should help the learner to obtain the information necessary to write a specific text in the target language and to adhere to the adequate text format of the other culture. This multicultural writing tool, which already exists as a prototype, contains textual information about five European languages, Danish, German, English, French and Portuguese. For financial reasons, the final version of the program will contain only information about two text types, curriculum vitae and letter of application.

Data collection for this program took a long time and was based on various sources. We consulted handbooks, which are quite numerous in the case of these text types. We also looked into collections of authentic curricula vitae and letters of application which were put at our disposal by business firms in the different countries. We asked experts for information, especially ESP experts and teachers who teach languages for specific purposes. Finally we interviewed the heads of the personnel offices of large firms and asked them about the criteria for good curricula vitae and letters of application.

The program which we developed on the basis of the information obtained is a database structured according to hypertext principles. Programming was done in TOOLBOOK. We tried to design our program according to the principles of cognitive tools as discussed in this paper. I will mention some of the features:

1. The user is presented with different ways to write a letter of application or a curriculum vitae. But he has to decide himself, based on his own personal

parameters, which way he chooses. Put more abstractly: different ways to solve a problem are presented; the user is asked to choose the right one by himself.

2.   The database contains a multitude of examples which are presented for different levels. The user can make use of them, but need not do so. The multitude of data and at the same time the user's freedom to decide which data to choose should help him organise his own knowledge construction in the way he thinks is right.

3.   The learner has the option to formulate his letter of application or his curriculum vitae within the program. For this purpose he has all the facilities of a word processor at his disposal. However, he cannot use the copy function to copy example sentences, formulae or whole texts out of the program into his own text. Although this would be technically possible, we rejected this option. A program which can be used to put together a text without knowing the language is neither a learning tool nor a cognitive tool to promote second language writing.

4.   We are trying to build a kind of mind map into the program which will help learners to get some orientation as to where they are in the program and which allows them to move on to any other part of the program. This mind map will also make it possible for learners to follow retrospectively the ways and means they exploited while producing the text.

Conclusion

I cannot go into any further detail here about the possibilities of using the computer as a cognitive tool in the foreign language classroom. Let me conclude by repeating its most important functions in learning: the computer can make the learner more conscious of information processing and learning and thus develop knowledge construction. It can provide classificatory help and thus make knowledge construction more transparent. And it can provide prestructured information and thus facilitate the organisation of the knowledge construction process.

References

Eck, A./Legenhausen, L./Wolff, D. (1994): "Der Einsatz der Telekommunikation in einem lernerorientierten Fremdsprachenunterricht". In: Gienow, W./Hellwig, K.H. (eds.): *Interkulturelle Kommunikation und prozeßorientierte Medienpraxis im Fremdsprachenunterricht: Grundlagen - Realisierung - Wirksamkeit.* Velber, Friedrich, pp. 43-57.
Eck, A./Legenhausen, L./Wolff, D. (1995): *Telekommunikation und Fremdsprachenunterricht: Informationen, Projekte, Ergebnisse.* Bochum, AKS-Verlag.
Jonassen, D. (1992): "Evaluating Constructivistic Learning". In: Duffy, T.M./Jonassen, D.H. (eds.): *Constructivism and the Technology of Instruction: A Conversation.* Hillsdale, N.J., Erlbaum, pp. 137-148.
Kelly, G. (1963): *A Theory of Personality.* New York, Norton.

Kommers, P.A.M. (1992): "Cognitive Tools: Prospects for Exploratory Learning Environments". In: Kommers, P.A.M./Jonassen, D.H./Mayes, J.T. (eds.): *Cognitive Tools for Learning*. Berlin, Springer, v-vi.

Legenhausen, L./Wolff, D. (1991): "Der Micro-Computer als Hilfsmittel beim Sprachenlernen: Schreiben als Gruppenaktivität". In: *Praxis des Neusprachlichen Unterrichts* 38, pp. 346-356.

Mercer, N. (1995): *The Guided Construction of Knowledge*. Clevedon: Multilingual Matters.

Rumelhart, D.E./Norman, D.A. (1978): "Accretion, Tuning and Restructuring". In: Cotton, J.W./Klatzky, R. (eds.): *Semantic Factors in Cognition*. Hillsdale, N.J., Erlbaum.

Sharples, M. (1988): "Back Words". In: *Computers and Writing Newsletter* 1, 15.

Wolff, D. (1994a): "Computers in Classroom Research". *Computers in Education* 23, pp. 133-142.

Wolff, D. (1994b): "Der Konstruktivismus: Ein neues Paradigma in der Fremdsprachendidaktik?" *Die Neueren Sprachen* 93, pp. 407-429.

2. LESSONS FROM THE PAST, LESSONS FOR THE FUTURE: 20 YEARS OF *CALL*

Graham DAVIES - United Kingdom

Plus ça change, plus c'est la même chose

This article is a personal view of the developments I have seen in the course of 20 years' involvement in CALL and more than 30 years' involvement in language teaching and learning technology. Looking back over the last 20 years, it seems to be a case of *plus ça change, plus c'est la même chose*. Yet it need not be like that. We desperately need new ideas in CALL, but it is equally important that newcomers to CALL learn from the lessons of the past.

Dynamic obsolescence

In January 1993 a conference on Foreign Language Learning and the Use of New Technologies was held in London, organised under the auspices of the European Commission's Lingua Bureau and the DELTA Programme. At the last minute I was invited to express my views on the use of technology in a higher education language centre, and in the course of my impromptu talk I threw in the phrase "dynamic obsolescence" in a reference to the problem of hardware and software constantly becoming out of date. The phrase was subsequently quoted in the proceedings (EC Lingua Bureau/DELTA 1993:120). I felt a bit guilty about that as I knew the phrase was not my own coinage, but I could not remember at the time where I had read or heard it. When I was commissioned to contribute to this volume, the penny dropped. I had read the phrase in a collection of articles by the British humorist Alan Coren, the paperback edition having been published, significantly, in the year when I embarked upon my new career as a language technologist: 1976. The context is worth quoting in full as it is highly relevant to the problems we face in language technology:

> "A number of my contemporaries actually chose to go into the Foreign Office: if they read Arabic at university, they were swooped on by Whitehall and sent to Japan; if they read Japanese, they were sent on a special FO training course to learn German, and subsequently placed in Kampala; if their predilection and brilliance were commercial, they were given posts where political expertise was the sole requirement; if they were geographers, they were despatched to found hospitals or advise on fowl pest. In short, as soon as they had completed the long and arduous process of learning something, it was no longer required. They were in a state of permanent dynamic obsolescence. My entire life has been like that." (Coren 1976:11)

I share Alan Coren's feelings. As a medieval Germanist, turned modern German language teacher, turned language technologist, most of my life has been like that,

27

especially the last 20 years - which brings me to the first lesson we can learn from the past.

Lesson No. 1: The language lab: training is an ongoing process

It is not uncommon for training to be given a low priority. This is true both of the business and of the education sector. There is a prevailing myth that once someone has been on a training course they need never go on another one. We all know this is nonsense, but unfortunately this cuts little ice with the accountants, who are only too aware that the training budget is one of the easiest to cut. There is also a naive belief that sending a language teacher on a general training course in the use of computers is sufficient. This is also nonsense. Training must be an ongoing process, and language teachers need properly tailored courses.

Here we can learn a lot from the past. Lack of training sounded the death-knell of the language lab. I belong to the generation that was trained in the early 1960s, when the reel-to-reel tape recorder and the film strip projector were the main technological aids that the language teacher used - if at all - and the language lab was the latest form of technology the new generation might expect to use - which we got quite excited about. The 1960s and 1970s saw a rapid growth in language labs, bolstered by the then fashionable audiolingual approach to language teaching, followed by a rapid decline. Why the growth and why the decline?

(i)   Reasons for the growth of the language lab:

    ·   Belief in technology as the panacea
    ·   Belief in "control"

(ii) Reasons for the decline of the language lab:

    ·   Technology failed to deliver what was expected
    ·   "Control" went out of fashion
    ·   Unreliable
    ·   Not user-friendly
    ·   The "battery chicken syndrome"
    ·   Lack of training: operation
    ·   Lack of training: methodology
    ·   Lack of materials
    ·   Lack of time
    ·   Lack of ideas

These are important points that should serve as lessons for the future, and I shall return to them later.

As the language lab declined in popularity, microcomputers began to gain wider penetration into the education sector. At last schools could afford them, but there was already an inherent danger that the microcomputer would go the same way as the

28

technology that preceded it. This problem was addressed in the UK by CILT, the Centre for Information on Language Teaching and Research. In 1982, CILT organised its first workshop on computing for language teachers at St Martin's College, Lancaster, and in the same year commissioned John Higgins and myself to write an introductory booklet on the use of computers in language learning (Davies & Higgins 1982). I shall continually refer to this booklet, as both John Higgins and I identified many needs and trends that represent a yardstick against which the current situation can be measured.

CILT's 1982 workshop was a successful event, and similar workshops - changing in tune with the changing face of computing and the modern foreign languages curriculum - have taken place every year to date. At a European level, the Council of Europe's new-style Workshops 7A, 7B, 9A and 9B (1991-1995) were also an important step in the right direction. In these workshops, participants from all over Europe were offered a mixed programme consisting of lectures, software presentations, show-and-tell sessions and, importantly, a large amount of time devoted to group work[1]. More of the same is the future recipe for success.

The ingredient missing from the training recipe at present is CALL methodology. One cannot avoid thinking that to a large extent language teachers and teacher trainers have not come to terms with CALL methodology. Is there in fact an emerging CALL methodology? The answer is probably "yes", and a forthcoming publication by Oxford University Press, based on research carried out by Michael Levy, University of Queensland, Australia, will provide some of the answers (Levy 1996). Training in CALL methodology will help us avoid some of the mistakes of the past.

Lesson No. 2: Technology is not the panacea

Although it can be clearly demonstrated that technology alone has cured few problems in the past, there appears to be a persistent refusal on the part of both administrators and technologists to accept this rather obvious fact. Language teachers are now confronted with a three-pronged attack: from the administrators, from the technologists, and from the guardians of the new technology.

Beware of the administrator

In the 1990s we are faced with increasing numbers of students of languages at all levels, with a static or declining number of teachers. The "battery chicken syndrome", to which I referred above in the context of the introduction of the language lab, is once again rearing its head. In the 1960s many educational administrators believed that teaching time could be saved by the battery-farming approach: put the students into the booths, connect them to the headsets, switch on the lab, and in a few weeks they'll be ready for the market. All the teacher had to do was sit at the console and monitor their progress. Inherent in this perception of mass training was the concept of technology as

---

[1]   Reports on Workshops 7A, 7B, 9A and 9B are available from the Council of Europe.

the panacea. It didn't work, of course. The students were cut off from one another in the language lab booths in the same way as the unfortunate chickens who spend their short, isolated lives in battery farms. The problem is still with us and eloquently dealt with by Sue Otto in a reference to what she calls the "isolative potential of technology" (Otto 1993:9-10).

The typical administrator's perception of mass education is illustrated by Sue Otto in a significant remark by a Dean of Faculty:

> "By next fall we want you to have complete multimedia courseware up and running for all five languages. And could you please tell me by how many people I can reduce the language teaching staff once these materials are in place." (Otto 1993:16)

The reader may by now have come to the conclusion that Sue Otto and I are natural-born Luddites. This is not true. Technology in the language classroom has its place; it is a useful support and enhancement but cannot replace human interaction. And technology is not necessarily a cheap solution; in fact it may prove more expensive, especially in the initial stages.

Technology can improve the quality of the learning environment by offering the student a variety of stimulating media, and it is essential in a self-access centre. But technology in education can only be effective when both the teachers and the administrators understand what it is all about, make the right purchasing decisions and embark upon a proper programme of awareness-raising and training. As Sue Otto points out, once the language teachers have been trained they need to educate the administrators (Otto 1993:16-17).

Beware of the trainspotter

Administrators represent one kind of threat to the language teacher, because they believe that throwing hardware at a problem will save money. The trainspotters of the computer world - also known as "anoraks" or "tekkies" in some circles - represent a different kind of threat, because of their belief in technology for technology's sake. Trainspotting is a hobby that does not seem to be widespread outside the UK, and my colleagues in Continental Europe often raise their eyebrows when I refer to trainspotters in the context of computing. I have never understood the attraction of this hobby. Essentially, it appears to be an obsession with trains as pieces of machinery. The purpose for which trains were designed, i.e. moving people from A to B, appears to be of minor importance.

One of the ways in which the trainspotter's fascination with technology manifests itself is an obsession with gimmicks and a desire to make use of them regardless of their pedagogical relevance. For example, most computers in the early 1980s were incapable of producing high-quality, unambiguous images, but this did not prevent programmers from introducing graphics into their programs at every opportunity (Davies & Higgins 1982:19, Davies & Higgins 1985:35-36). Graphics are of course much better now, and

30

the reproduction of a full-colour photograph on a modern computer is not a problem, but we can see the same old mistake being made with motion video. Most multimedia PCs in educational institutions are still incapable of running video at an acceptable speed of at least 25 frames per second, i.e. the speed at which lip synchronisation with the soundtrack looks right, but I have seen numerous examples of talking heads, with the lips and facial gestures poorly synchronised with the sound, that bring few benefits. Ironically, the appearance of the multimedia PC caused designers of CALL programs incorporating motion video to take a step backwards, as interactive video (IV) systems were well developed as long ago as the early 1980s (Davies & Higgins 1982:23-24). This is a typical case of new technology driving the pedagogy. The older IV systems consisted of a computer linked to a Philips-compatible 12-inch laserdisc player, and they offered high-quality, full-motion video that was ideally suited to CALL. During the 1980s many interactive videodiscs were produced, for example *Expodisc*[1] and the *Connections* series[2]. Such packages allowed the user to switch subtitles on and off at will and participate in dialogues, even recording his/her own voice and matching it with a native speaker model. Unfortunately, this combination of hardware did not prove popular and the consequence is that interactive videodiscs did not reach the wider audience that they deserved. Nevertheless, interactive videodiscs are still being produced for this outdated hardware combination[3]. As for the future, we have to wait for multimedia PCs with faster video interfaces, e.g. MPEG, in order to get back to the standards we came to expect in the 1980s.

Speech synthesis is another example of the inappropriate use of technology. Few language teachers were impressed by the synthetic voices that were introduced into CALL programs in the 1980s. The demand for authenticity was too well established, and language teachers could not be persuaded that a voice sounding like a robot was a good model to imitate (Davies & Higgins 1982:55-56). At the time it was not easy to produce authentic speech on a computer. Various devices that attempted to link computers with tape recorders were too cumbersome to be practical (ibid.), and synthetic voices were used as a convenient, though inappropriate, solution. Nowadays all multimedia computers are capable of producing high-quality authentic digitised speech, and I thought that speech synthesis - although now much improved - was unlikely to raise its head again in the context of CALL. I was wrong: in 1994 I found

---

[1]   *Expodisc* is marketed by Multi Media Training, Marcom House, 1 Heathlands, Heath Gardens, Twickenham, Middlesex TW1 4BP, UK, Tel +44 181 744 1624. See Davies, G. D. (1991).

[2]   The *Connections* series is now being reversioned to run on MPCs equipped with an MPEG card. Further details from Vektor Ltd, The Oaks, Preston Road, Chorley, Lancs PR7 1PL, UK, Tel +44 1257 232222, Fax +44 1257 234039.

[3]   In a survey of the use of new technologies in language training that I supervised on behalf of the EC's Lingua Bureau in 1994, two interactive videodisc development projects were examined: Lingua Project No. 92-09/0752/E-III and Lingua Project No. 93-09/1188/DK-III (Davies, Bangs & Betts 1994:8-9 & 35-36).

a synthetic voice being used in a pronouncing dictionary that formed part of a CD-ROM for learners of English as a Foreign Language.[1]

Automatic speech recognition (ASR) is another contentious area of CALL. ASR is now being integrated into many CALL programs, two of which I have listed at the end of this article. I have been favourably impressed by some ASR software, but it is still primitive compared with the human ear. The teacher is by far the better judge of the acceptability of pronunciation, and what is wrong with training the student to listen to his/her own voice and to make his/her own judgements? It appears that ASR is favoured most by those who believe in control.

Finally, let us consider the graphical user interface (GUI) as found on the Apple Mac and in Windows on the PC. There is little doubt that GUIs have made life much easier for computer users. Few people would disagree that pointing and clicking with a mouse is a major improvement on having to memorise very unmemorable DOS commands. But what we have seen in recent years is a veritable explosion of CALL programs in which all the learner has to do is point and click, often with the minimum of mental processing. For example, I managed to work my way through the first part of a program for learners of Japanese without understanding a word of the language. Keyboard input and discrete feedback have been abandoned, and interactivity is reduced to a selection from choices. In other words, many CALL programs have turned into true/false and multiple-choice exercises - a "very active way of being passive", as a young language teacher was recently heard to remark at a recent conference where a new CD-ROM was being presented. I have always been under the impression that part of the process of learning a language involves committing to memory totally unmemorable foreign words and phrases - in suitable contexts, of course - and I find it curious that few modern CALL programs test the learner's ability to demonstrate his/her ability to recall what he/she has learned, either in written or spoken form.

The Empire Strikes Back

A consequence of the advent of the microcomputer in the early 1980s was that computer users' control of their destiny was wrested from the men (rarely women) in white coats who ran mainframe computing centres. But this process of devolution of power to the people was short-lived. The men in white coats, now accompanied by more women in similar attire, reappeared, this time in the guise of local area network managers. The local area network (LAN) is popular with administrators because it is perceived as a means of saving money, e.g. it is possible to negotiate low-cost network licences for commonly used software. There is no doubt that LANs have their advantages. They overcome the problems - and costs - of issuing dozens of floppy disks to clumsy students, but running a LAN requires a high level of training and a lot of time, and this fact is rarely appreciated by the administrators. As a result, LAN managers are often teachers who have been on a one-day training course and only know the basic network commands without any theoretical knowledge of the concepts. A good

---

[1]   Lingua Project No. 93-09/1278/I-III (Davies, Bangs & Betts 1994:43-44).

LAN manager is indispensable, but too many lack the knowledge to run a network efficiently. And those who do have the knowledge all too often adopt a gatekeeper mentality when anyone encroaches on their territory and dares to suggest that network technology is not the panacea it is perceived to be. For example, LANs demonstrate major shortcomings in handling CD-ROMs. The key problem has been succinctly summarised by David Eastment:

"It is difficult to see how CD-ROM could be used effectively in a conventional Computer Room. Networking CD-ROMs is fine for simple text. But sending video and audio information around the net so that it finishes up perfectly synchronised at each user's workstation is fraught with difficulties. The alternative is to set up each of the student stations as multimedia machines with their own CD-ROM drives, and provide each station with the CD-ROM discs it needs. It is problematic enough working like this from floppy disk, where at least you can copy the information on to multiple copies and keep your master safe. Working with CD means that every single workstation would have to have its own original CD-ROM disc in place, Frankly, I cannot imagine many schools going down this path. Soon, perhaps, the technical problems will be solved, or new software will emerge which will prove more 'classroom-friendly'. For the moment, however, CD-ROM is likely to be confined either to individuals or to small groups at a single PC." (Eastment 1994:75)

My own experience supports this view. In the course of 1994-95 I was invited by 20 different educational institutions in the UK and in Continental Europe to give presentations on the use of CD-ROMs in language learning and teaching. Out of the 20 institutions that I visited, only two were able to supply me immediately with hardware that had been set up correctly. A recurrent problem was that LAN managers were unaware that many CALL programs on CD-ROM make extensive use of the playback and recording of sound in combination with elaborate graphics, e.g. the role-plays in the program *TriplePlay Plus*, which I describe at the end of this article. Such programs do not work successfully on LANs - at least not on the type of LANs that are installed in most educational institutions. Fortunately, for all but one of my presentations I was able to find stand-alone multimedia PCs that could be persuaded to work - after considerable intervention by local technicians.

So what is the solution? David Eastment provides one possible answer: each networked workstation has to have its own CD-ROM drive, and I know of several universities that have recognised that this configuration is a viable solution. The bonus in adopting this approach is that each workstation can then double as an audio CD player - an enormous advantage now that many language courses are available on audio CD. But this is a luxury most educational institutions cannot afford. The result is that the only CD-ROM software that will work efficiently on LANs in most educational institutions lacks the kind of interactivity that language teachers have come to expect. The message that I continually receive from language teachers is one of frustration at not being able to use up-to-date software because of a decision having been made to "network everything".

Lesson No. 3: Don't back the wrong horse

In 1982 I wrote:

> "Generally speaking, it is a good idea to choose a popular established microcomputer rather than a very new or obscure machine. There are two sound reasons for doing so: First, an extensive range of software is likely to be available for a machine which has been around for a while. Second, the more widely known the machine, the easier it will be to obtain advice on using it and to get it serviced." (Davies & Higgins 1982:51)

It is surprising how many people ignore this advice. Making a new hardware purchase can be an expensive gamble. The past is littered with dead hardware. In the 1960s and 1970s we had reel-to-reel audio tapes, eight-track cassettes, single-spool Philips cassettes and dual-spool Philips cassettes. Eventually, the dual-spool Philips cassette won the race, and this is probably the only type of audiocassette with which young people are familiar. A similar race between Betamax and VHS videocassettes took place. Betamax was better than VHS but it came in second. Similarly, the first Apple Mac was unquestionably a superior machine compared to the early PC, but PCs now outnumber Apple Macs by an enormous margin.

The unstable state of hardware presents users of CALL packages with difficult choices, but designers face a nightmare scenario. On the one hand, they wish to produce packages which are both pedagogically sound and make the best use of new technology. On the other hand, the technology which suits their needs will not necessarily become widely available, and they will then be deprived of a market for their products. For example, in the late 1970s the first *CLEF* programs were written for learners of French (Holmes & Kidd 1980). The designers wished to avoid reproducing a textbook on screen and they were committed to the use of colour, animation and graphics, which they felt made better use of the computer's facilities. The only microcomputer that could cope with their demands at the time was the Compucolor. The programs looked good on this machine and were ahead of their time in both concept and design, but it was the wrong hardware choice. The Compucolor did not sell, and the *CLEF* programs had to be rewritten for a series of machines: the Commodore PET, the Commodore 64 and the first IBM-compatible PC. A lot of effort was therefore wasted. Similarly, those of us who were committed to incorporating sound into our programs struggled with hardware such as Tandberg's AECAL system (Davies & Higgins 1982:55-56, Davies & Higgins 1985:33, 92). Our efforts were also in vain, as such systems were short-lived. As I have already indicated in the previous section (Lesson No. 2), IV systems based on the Philips laserdisc player did not prove popular, even though the quality of the motion video that 12-inch videodiscs offered was first-rate, and certainly superior to what is found today on most CD-ROMs.

So what is the solution? The answer is to be patient, assess which way the market is moving and focus on the hardware most people in your sector are using. CDI systems have been publicised widely over the last few years, and the quality of the motion video such systems offer is impressive. I remain cautious, however, as I have not noticed language centres rushing out to buy CDI equipment.

Once you have made the choice of hardware, you then have to choose the software. The operating system will probably have been pre-installed, but decisions on applications software will have to be made, and at a later stage upgrades will have to be considered. This is a minefield I do not propose to enter. I shall limit myself to one observation:

The educational sector is slow to replace hardware, and computers over five years old are common in both schools and universities. It is also quite likely that the department that gets the new hardware is a computer unit or IT department, which then dumps its obsolete machines on the unfortunate languages departments. CALL software developers are aware of this fact and therefore do not rush to produce software that will run on the latest equipment. Two CALL software producers and retailers, Camsoft and Wida Software, report that DOS programs are still outselling Windows programs both in the UK and abroad.[1]

Lesson No. 4: A little bit of control is enough

I have already referred to the question of control: the belief in control as a general principle, the teacher at the control console in the language lab, and the LAN manager controlling the network server. I addressed the issue of the computer controlling the learner in 1992, in an article I wrote for language trainers in the business sector:

> "A business trainee is sitting at a computer following a language course. Step-by-step, the computer presents the essential vocabulary and structures. These are accompanied, where appropriate, by still and animated graphic images, photographs and video recordings. As new words and phrases are introduced, authentic male and female voices pronounce them and the learner repeats them. The learner's voice is recorded by the computer and played back. Any errors in pronunciation are indicated graphically on screen. Offending syllables are highlighted and additional practice is offered on sounds which the learner finds difficult. At the end of each presentation sequence, the computer tests the learner's grasp of the new vocabulary and structures, marking and recording those words and phrases which have been imperfectly recalled and offering feedback on points of grammar that the learner appears to have misunderstood. The learner has access at all times to an on-line dictionary, a reference grammar and verb conjugation tables. At the end of the work session the learner's progress is recorded by the computer, which enables the thread to be picked up at the next session. In addition, the learner's progress records - along with those of all the other trainees following the same course - can be accessed at any time by the training manager." (Davies 1992:112)

---

[1]   Sources of information: (i) Sally Campbell, Camsoft, 10 Wheatfield Close, Maidenhead, Berks SL3 3PS, UK, Tel/Fax +44 1628 825206; (ii) Tony Williams, Wida Software, 2 Nicholas Gardens, London W5 5DX, Tel +44 181 567 6940, Fax +44 181 840 6534.

To some people this scenario is utopian, and to others it is a vision of hell. I suspected that business training managers might perceive it as utopian, but I was wrong: so far they have shown little interest in CALL in any form. My own position is suggested in the title to this section.

I was trained as a teacher when the audiolingual approach was in vogue and three-phase drills in the language lab were considered the best way for students to get their tongues round unfamiliar sounds and to fix sentence patterns in their heads. In other words, the approach was predominantly behaviouristic, with the teacher sitting firmly in control at the language lab console. This approach owed much to programmed learning.

Early CALL programs also owed much to programmed learning. I confess to having been initially fascinated by the idea of the computer reacting to the learner's input and branching accordingly, and I admit to having written many CALL routines that were unquestionably behaviouristic (Davies & Higgins 1982:8ff.). Many of the pioneers in CALL started that way, only gradually discovering that the computer lent itself to different approaches.[1] The early PLATO programs were based on a programmed learning approach, which appealed to some educators. In 1982 I attended the South African Congress on Computers in Education at the University of Stellenbosch. The Control Data Corporation was very much in evidence at this conference, making considerable efforts to establish its mainframe PLATO system in the coloured and black universities. The white administrators thought it was a good idea, as it appeared to solve the problem of teacher shortages and also enabled them to control the educational process. The venture was not a major success, and I recall the report of a teacher trainer in KwaZulu who completely lost faith in the system when it refused to allow a learner of English as a Foreign Language to progress further in a program because she had not reached the required level in a summative test - having made a two-hour journey by bus to the local college where the PLATO terminal was installed and having worked on the program for less than half an hour!

In the scenario I described at the beginning of this section, the machine is controlling the learning process. In this scenario I have created an imaginary "intelligent" CALL (ICALL) package - at least I think it is imaginary. ICALL leans heavily on techniques developed by specialists in Artificial Intelligence (AI), a term I have always considered to be a perfect example of an oxymoron. AI techniques have attracted a good deal of attention in CALL, but they have also come in for severe criticism.

Alan Turing was one of the first computer scientists to set up a yardstick for measuring machine intelligence: the famous "Turing Test", which hinges on the ability of the computer, or rather the set of instructions with which it has been programmed, to convince a person communicating with it via a remote terminal that it is a human being and not a machine (Turing 1964, Davies & Higgins 1982:28). The thinking machine is

---

[1] Levy's survey (Levy 1996) established that the majority of CALL program designers declared themselves to favour the communicative approach, but few language teachers could agree on what this meant.

a nice idea, but the Turing Test is not necessarily a measure of intelligence. The American philosopher John Searle attacked this idea in his articles on the "Chinese Room" (Searle 1980, Searle 1982). Searle's Chinese Room represents the computer. A human being may ask the Chinese Room questions in Chinese by posting them into the room in written form. The Chinese Room appears to understand Chinese as it is able to deliver written answers to the questions. What is happening, however, is that there is an operator inside the room who identifies each character in a dictionary and checks the rules of grammar and usage in order to ascertain the meaning of the question. He then assembles an answer, again by checking his dictionary and the rules of grammar and usage. He does not, however, understand Chinese; he is simply manipulating symbols according to a set of elaborate rules. In a BBC *Horizon* program, *Thinking*, first broadcast in 1987, Searle once more attacked the idea of rule-based skills:

> "If my dog can catch a ball that's bounced off the wall, that may be just a skill he's acquired. The alternative view (*the pro-AI view*) would say: 'Look, if the dog can catch the ball it can only be because he knows the rule: go to the point where the angle of incidence equals the angle of reflection in a plane where the flatness of the trajectory is a function of the impact velocity divided by the coefficient of friction' - or something like that. Now, it seems to me unreasonable to think that my dog really *knows* that. It seems to me more reasonable to suppose he just learns how to look for where the ball is going to and jumps *there*. And a lot of our behaviour is like that as well. We've acquired a lot of skills, but we don't have to suppose that, in order to acquire these skills, the skills have got to be based on our mastery of some complex intellectual structure. For an awful lot of things, we just *do* it."

Searle's articles on the Chinese Room attracted a large number of responses by supporters of AI, e.g. Harnad (1989), but I am not aware of a completely satisfactory answer to his criticism, particularly of what he calls "Strong AI", i.e. the idea that the human brain is just a set of electrons firing in different directions and that we only need to model this process in a computer program in order to produce an intelligent machine.

The key problem in programming a computer with the rules of natural language is that linguists do not fully understand the rules themselves, so they cannot give adequate instructions to computer programmers. As Searle says, "we just *do* it". It is clear to me that over the last 20 years AI has failed to make a major breakthrough in natural language processing. One only has to look at modern commercial grammar checkers and machine translation programs to see how much work still needs to be done. Research conducted into the effectiveness of a well-known grammar checker by one of my students, Yu Hong Wei, revealed an alarming number of examples of incorrect advice. The texts in square brackets in the following two examples were the grammar checker's reactions to the sentences in italics:

(i) *I just remember how excited I was.*
     [The subject pronoun "I" shouldn't be in the object position.]

(ii) *The government should work towards making parents aware about how to keep track of their children.*
[The adjective "aware" should come before the noun phrase "parents".]

A commercial machine translation program that promised "fast understandable translations" produced the following gems:

(i) "Defiance intensively efforts are it to the UN up to now not felicitous, to move the war-parties to a lengthening of the agreement."
(ii) "Survey becomes loudly the authorities of 62 more people."

Given the context of the first example, an article on the war in Bosnia, I was able to work out what this nonsense probably meant, but I had to go back to the source to reassure myself:

(i) *Trotz intensiver Bemühungen ist es der UNO bislang nicht gelungen, die Kriegsparteien zu einer Verlängerung des Abkommens zu bewegen.*
("In spite of intensive efforts, the United Nations have not succeeded in persuading the warring factions to extend their agreement.")

I was fooled totally by the second example, but a quick examination of the source revealed all:

(ii) *Vermißt werden laut den Behörden noch 62 Menschen.*
("According to the authorities, 62 people are still missing.")

One wonders whether accountants would be prepared to accept a similar lack of accuracy in a spreadsheet package.

Attempts to write CALL programs that can parse the learner's inputs at the keyboard and indicate whether the learner has constructed grammatically and semantically correct sentences have also failed. Programs that purport to be AI-based often turn out to be simple examples of programmed learning that check the student's responses against a set of acceptable answers and anticipated errors, offering appropriate feedback and branching accordingly - which may not necessarily be a bad thing if it is done well. The success or failure of this approach depends on the overall program design. The modern approach stresses the importance of *guidance* rather than *control*, offering the student a default route through the program as an alternative to browsing, and building in intrinsic rather than extrinsic feedback, so that the learner has a chance to identify his/her own mistakes (Laurillard 1993).

To come back to the scenario I described at the beginning of this section, the most worrying aspect of AI is the element of control that its supporters apparently wish to build into their programs. I shall leave the last word in this section to Rex Last, one of the pioneers in CALL, who devoted a whole book to AI in language learning, changing his mind in the process and coming to a very pessimistic conclusion:

"In going down this dangerous path, it seems to me that we are indeed seeking to marginalise humanity and create a race of computerised monsters which, when the power of decision-making is given into their hands, will decree that the human race, with its passions, inconsistencies, foibles and frailties, should be declared redundant, and that the intelligent machine shall inherit the earth. And that, fundamentally, is why my initial enthusiasm has now turned so sour." (Last 1989:153)

Lesson No. 5: Ideas are paramount

One of the reasons for the decline of the language lab that I indicated above (Lesson No. 1) was the lack of ideas. During the 1980s, however, the language lab was given a new lease of life. This was partly due to improved reliability, more user-friendly controls, more imaginative materials and improved lab design that got away from the battery-chicken-farm appearance of rows of booths. At the same time, self-access was coming into fashion and there was a wealth of new ideas on using the lab: pair work, group work, role-play, communication games, etc. (Ely 1984).

There has always been a danger that a lack of ideas might kill CALL. The problem lies not so much in the lack of imaginative programs, more in teachers' attitudes to CALL. Jones (1986) summarised the problem as follows:

"Language-learning computer programs, to a much greater extent than language-learning materials on paper, are expected to stand or fall on their own merits, without consideration of their role in a classroom lesson." (Jones 1986:171)

"Whereas the teacher and the textbook, or the teacher and the cassette recorder, are regarded as classroom allies, the computer and teacher have generally been seen more as rivals." (Jones 1986:171)

Such attitudes are probably due to the fact that teachers perceive the computer as controlling events in the language classroom or in the self-access room. No computer program stands or falls on its own merits, no more than any coursebook or audiocassette. All too often I have observed teachers dismissing a program as "rubbish", without giving the slightest consideration as to where it might fit into their classroom activities or as part of a guided self-access scheme. Most teachers can probably benefit from Jones' advice, which is just as valid today as it was ten years ago:

- Try it and see what happens. Don't pre-judge.
- Don't expect the program to do all the work.
- If things don't work out, don't automatically blame the program. The problem may lie elsewhere.
- Above all, use your imagination. (Jones 1986:178)

A good example of the imaginative use of a program - or type of program - is a technique which has come to be known as data-driven learning (DDL). The type of program to which I am referring is the concordance package - or concordancer.

39

Concordances were originally used by linguistic and literary researchers, and in the old days these were compiled manually. It used to be possible to be awarded a Master's Degree by compiling a concordance of an author's works, but this would not be allowed today as computers can do the work in a matter of hours.

The use of concordancing packages ties in with the concept of the lexical syllabus (Willis 1990). Tim Johns was one of the first teachers I saw making use of a concordancer in language teaching, using a package which he had written on a tiny Sinclair ZX81 computer in the early 1980s. This embryonic program went through several stages of development, eventually being published some ten years later by Oxford University Press as *MicroConcord*, a concordancer designed for language teachers that includes a good selection of optional text corpora. There are numerous ways in which the teacher can use a concordancer in the language classroom, for example:

· The teacher can use the concordancer to find examples of authentic usage to demonstrate a point of grammar, typical collocations, etc.
· The teacher can generate exercises based on examples drawn from a variety of corpora.
· Students can work out rules of grammar and usage for themselves by searching for key words in context.
· Students are encouraged to be sceptical about explicit rules.

More examples and a wealth of ideas are described by Tribble and Jones (1990), Johns (1991) and Johns & King (1991).

New ideas in CALL are slow to emerge but, as Nina Garrett points out, the computer offers us an excellent opportunity to "challenge the limitations of current pedagogy, the prescriptions, proscriptions, priorities, and a priori assumptions which up-to-date teachers accept as given" (Garrett 1991:17). The fact is that we don't know what goes on inside language learners' heads but, by tracking how learners behave - which is easily done, and is in fact being done at this moment by Vance Stevens, one of my research students - we might have a better understanding of the effectiveness of CALL activities and which learning strategies are desirable.

Lesson No. 6: Doing it yourself is not the answer

Writing your own materials sounds like a good idea, but few language teachers have the time to do so. When I embarked upon my career as a language technologist in the 1970s, I grappled with three programming languages: FORTRAN, SNOBOL and BASIC. When I got to grips with BASIC I was able to write a number of simple question-answer routines on Ealing College's minicomputer. I found programming each new routine tedious, however, and decided to speed up the process by writing an authoring facility. The complete package, which included both the teacher's and the student's programs, was published by Wida Software in 1981 as *Teacher's Toolkit*. The package was developed further and published by Hutchinson in 1982 under a new name: *Questionmaster* (Davies & Higgins 1985:64-66). *Questionmaster* was a simple tool, requiring the teacher to type in a question, a series of acceptable alternative answers and a hint to help the student to get on the right track. It soon became obvious, however, that teachers found this simple process too time-consuming, and there was a clear demand for ready-made materials to accompany the authoring package. The outcome was the production of *Apfeldeutsch*, which was created with *Questionmaster* and published by Wida Software in 1981. The demand for ready-made materials to accompany authoring packages is just as strong today as it was in the early 1980s, which accounts for the continuing popularity of Wida Software's *CALL for English* series and Camsoft's series of titles that tie in with Mary Glasgow's and Thomas Nelson's French, German and Spanish coursebooks.

The do-it-yourself approach to CALL software creation has rarely worked. Only those with hours of dedication at their disposal have made a success of it. The past is littered with dead authoring packages: *TES/T*, *Pilot*, *Microtext*, *TenCore*, etc. BASIC was simply too difficult for most language teachers. I was wrong to suggest that linguists might wish to become programmers (Davies & Higgins 1982:45) and foolish enough to devote a whole textbook to programming for users of language (Davies 1985) - which was not a bestseller. I still believe, however, that linguists who need to communicate with programmers ought to understand the way programs work. In 1982 I wrote, "The elegant solution to software creation is collaboration between linguists and programmers." (Davies & Higgins 1982:44). I have no reason to change my mind, and I firmly believe the best CALL software development team consists of two people: a linguist who understands something about programming and a programmer who understands something about language.

There are, however, two authoring programs which are enjoying continuing success today after a very long run: *Fun with Texts* (first published by Camsoft in 1985) and *Storyboard* (first published by Wida Software in 1982). Both enable the generation of total-text reconstruction exercises. Why have they lasted so long? One reason is that these programs generate the maximum of student activity with the minimum of effort on the part of the teacher: all the teacher has to do is find a text, type it - or copy and paste it if it already exists in electronic format - and store it on disk. The text then forms the basis of an activity that will keep the student busy for at least half an hour - or longer in the case of *Fun with Texts*, which generates seven different text-reconstruction exercises from one text. It was established by Sue Hewer, who based part of her (unpublished) MPhil thesis on a study of *CopyWrite*, a forerunner to *Fun with Texts*, that in a 30-minute session at the keyboard an average number of 128 input attempts took place when a group of three students collaborated on a total-text reconstruction exercise. Her research also established that an average number of 64.5 "strategy events" (i.e. group decision-making processes while handling the inputs) took place.[1] So the students were kept active, and a significant amount of discussion, negotiation and mental processing took place. Both Camsoft and Wida Software report

---

[1]   Personal communication by Sue Hewer, formerly a language teacher and now a free-lance CALL consultant.

that these two programs are still their bestsellers. It has been suggested that another reason for the popularity of these programs is that they appeal to LAN managers, because they run under DOS and are therefore easy to set up, and - unlike some Windows programs - cannot easily be tampered with by students[1].

Some authoring packages are useful for presentations and creating simple point-and-click routines, e.g. *Toolbook*, and these are fairly easy to learn. Others, e.g. *AuthorWare* and *Director*, are far too difficult for the amateur, and time-consuming even for the professional programmer - I speak from bitter experience. What the language teacher needs is a very basic authoring tool that requires the minimum of effort. I have recently been developing such a tool, which will enable the teacher to generate basic fill-in-the-blank and multiple-choice exercises - with or without sound and pictures. This is being released under the name *GapKit 2.0* and aims to provide a simple solution to multimedia authoring. This package presupposes knowledge only of Windows, in particular the accessories *Write*, *Paintbrush* and *Sound Recorder*.

Lesson No. 7: The Internet: beware of the hype

I have been using electronic mail (e-mail) for the last ten years. I check my three electronic mailboxes daily and deal with approximately 70 e-mail messages a week. I make extensive use of the Internet and used it in order to locate some of the sources of information that I have cited in this article. In a talk I first gave at the London Language Show in October 1995, I made two provocative statements about the Internet:

(i) "The Internet is a rich resource of material, accessible to everybody and of immense educational value."
(ii) "The Internet is a chaotic collection of material, most of which is junk and accessible only to the 5% of people in the world who possess a telephone. It is growing too rapidly, currently doubling in size every 55 days. It is impractical to use in an educational context and completely confusing to the novice. It's rather like having the British Library in your study with the prospect of four pantechnicons full of books being dumped on your doorstep every day."

The truth is somewhere in between. What can the language teacher realistically expect from the Internet?

From the early 1980s onwards we saw an explosion in hypertext programs. These appeared first on the Apple Mac and then on the PC. Most reference works on CD-ROM are now based on the hypertext principle. The idea of non-sequential reading, pointing and clicking anywhere on the screen and branching to wherever you like - known as browsing - has enormous appeal. Now we have the World Wide Web

---

[1]   Sources of information: (i) Sally Campbell, Camsoft, 10 Wheatfield Close, Maidenhead, Berks SL3 3PS, UK, Tel/Fax +44 1628 825206; (ii) Tony Williams, Wida Software, 2 Nicholas Gardens, London W5 5DX, Tel +44 181 567 6940, Fax +44 181 840 6534.

(WWW), effectively a world-wide hypertext system that enables the user to branch to any computer anywhere in the world simply by pointing and clicking at a piece of text or a picture.

The problem with browsing, whether it is in the context of a stand-alone hypertext stack or over the whole of the World Wide Web, is that it is *unstructured*. One learns in different ways, of course, sometimes by following a tightly structured course and sometimes by coming across a piece of interesting information completely by chance. If you have unlimited time, unstructured browsing is a very pleasant way of learning, but most people, especially those following courses in educational institutions, cannot afford to waste too much time on this activity. A certain amount of browsing is to be encouraged, and I firmly believe in allowing the learner to follow his/her own inclinations as far as is possible. Software, however, needs to offer what has become known in CALL jargon as the *default route*. Diana Laurillard puts the argument succinctly, as follows:

> "A default route is the route through the material that the author believes to be optimal. Completely open-ended program structure can make students anxious - they like to know what they are supposed to do. It must always be possible to deviate from the default route, but it should be clear what it is, so that they can just follow it through. This saves students having to make decisions at every turn, and may also encourage them to consolidate, rather than keep moving on."
> (Laurillard 1993:2)

In the context of telematics, it is important that students know what they are supposed to do. The ELNET computer conferencing project (1989-91), in which I participated as evaluator, was an imaginative experiment in linking together 15 educational institutions in three countries: England, France and Germany. As a language learning project, it suffered on the whole from a lack of control on the part of the teachers. Students would send one another messages on an ad hoc basis, most of which had little value as authentic language learning material. An "interventionist" approach (Davies, R. 1990:70) was therefore adopted halfway through the project, and this proved more effective, especially in teacher-monitored simulations:

> "It became apparent at the ELNET Conference in Würzburg, October 1991, that the success of one of the winners of this competition (*the Eurodesk multilingual business simulation*) was clearly due to a very tightly managed series of classroom activities which took place off-line while the simulation was running."
> (Davies, R. 1990:78).

The pedagogical argument regarding the balance between structured tasks and unstructured communication and browsing activities comes down heavily in favour of the former in the context of telematics, which can be a very expensive medium to maintain if control of the use of the access lines is not carefully monitored.

Most schools access the Internet via a modem and a standard narrowband telephone line. I access the Internet from my own home in this way, using a 14,400 bps modem that connects me with a local service provider. This setup is fine for sending e-mail messages and uploading and downloading text. However, I recently conducted a little experiment in downloading a variety of files:

(i)   A compressed reproduction of a colour photograph took three minutes to download.
(ii) A 25-page article took five minutes to download.
(iii) A single spoken sentence took five minutes to download.
(iv) A 2.5Mb program took one and a half hours to download. (I was able to use this time fruitfully by making a cup of coffee, marking a student's essay, taking my dog for a one-mile walk and watching the evening news broadcast on TV.)

At this rate a full CD-ROM would take about two weeks to download! Perhaps this is why many people think the initials WWW stand for World Wide Wait!

Universities access the Internet via their own systems, using special broadband lines that operate at a significantly higher speed than standard telephone lines. Real speed of access for everyone will only be possible when we can tap into fibre-optic communications systems, and that depends on individual countries' policies on telecommunications and how quickly the cable companies are able to dig up the roads and put the cables in place.

There is another snag: download times are dependent on how quickly the server (i.e. the computer) at the other end of the line copes with your demands. Accessing the Internet is rather like driving along a fast motorway and then being held up by a traffic jam for 45 minutes - rather like the trip from Munich to Salzburg on a Friday afternoon during the skiing season. If a lot of people wish to access a particular Web site at once, then a bottleneck ensues. The so-called Superhighway turns into a dirt-track after 11.30 am, i.e. when the USA begins to wake up. While trying to download an article from a UK server at the peak period of 2.00 pm, I spent 25 fruitless minutes waiting for it to present me with only 14% of the text. The best time proved to be 1.30 in the morning, the whole process taking only five minutes. Just out of curiosity, I accessed the same article from one of my university's Internet workstations at 3.30 pm the following day. This time the whole process took barely one minute. Such is the unpredictability of the Internet.

However, in spite of this gloomy and confusing picture it is fair to say that the World Wide Web offers a wealth of resources - mainly text - that can easily be accessed using basic equipment. The press in various languages is there, and so are encyclopaedias and a host of other reference works. Access does, however, need to be controlled in order to keep the bills to a minimum and to prevent students (and staff) downloading undesirable material.

EFL teachers have access to a vast range of resources, a good selection of which have been documented by David Eastment (1996). Teachers of other languages have access to fewer materials, sadly because the language of the Internet is predominantly English, but a search under terms in French, German and Spanish will usually locate the appropriate source.

My own selection of useful sites as starting points for links to masses of other sites for teachers and learners of languages are documented below:

- One of the fastest search engines on the Web is:
  http://www.altavista.digital.com/

- EUROCALL, European Association for Computer Assisted Language Learning:
  http://www.cti.hull.ac.uk/eurocall.htm

- A "Virtual Language Centre", currently being set up by NCET and CILT INTEH UK:
  http://ncet.csv.warwick.ac.uk/WWW/temps/linguanet/index.html

- Liverpool John Moores University World Language Pages:
  http://www.livjm.ac.uk/language/

- CALICO, Computer Assisted Language Instruction Consortium, USA:
  http://agoralang.com/calico.html

- IATEFL, International Association of English as a Foreign Language:
  http://www.man.ac.uk/IATEFL/

- Information on corpora and concordancing
  http://www.ruf.rice.edu/~barlow/corpus.html

Conclusion 1: Training and information are vital

I have already referred to the CILT's training workshops and the Council of Europe's new-style Workshops (Lesson No. 1). It is worth making the point again that training language teachers in specialised workshops and seminars on the use of new technology needs to be an ongoing process. Language teachers are better equipped than other teachers to benefit from international initiatives, on the grounds that they can communicate better with one another and probably have more of an inclination to work in international environments. The European Association for Computer Assisted Language Learning (EUROCALL) has been organising international conferences on CALL since the mid-1980s. More recently, EUROCALL has set up a database of international experts who are prepared to contribute to local workshops anywhere in Europe. Two such workshops have already taken place: Leuven, Belgium, May 1995; Mons, Belgium, December 1995.

Training needs to be backed up by access to relevant sources of information that enable teachers to keep up to date. EUROCALL is the main European organisation that is responsible for the dissemination of information on CALL. This is done electronically (see EUROCALL's Web site, detailed above), through conferences and through printed materials: *ReCALL Journal*, the *ReCALL Newsletter*, the *EUROCALL Newsletter*, etc. Further details are available from:

Mrs June Thompson
EUROCALL Secretary
CTI Centre for Modern Languages
University of Hull
UK- Hull - HU6 7DX
Tel +44 1482 466373
Fax +44 1482 473816
e-mail: eurocall@hull.ac.uk

The European Union is also devoting a substantial amount of funding to the promotion of training and development initiatives in new technologies and language learning under the Socrates, Leonardo and Fourth Framework programmes. Details are available from:

SOCRATES & Youth TAO/BAT
70 rue Montoyer
B-1040 Bruxelles
Tel +32 2 233 01 11
Fax +32 2 233 01 50

LEONARDO TAO/BAT
9 avenue de l'Astronomie
B-1210 Bruxelles
Tel +32 2 227 01 00
Fax +32 2 227 01 01

Telematics Applications Programme Helpdesk
Fourth R & D Framework Programme
DG XIII - C
200 rue de la Loi (BU29 4/81)
B-1049 Bruxelles
Tel +32 2 295 45 60
Fax +32 2 296 23 54

Conclusion 2: CD-ROM is the way ahead

At present it looks as if CD-ROM is the most promising way ahead. In spite of the shortcomings I have indicated regarding the quality of motion video on CD-ROM, I am confident that in the near future these problems will be overcome; in fact they have already been overcome, but the bulk of end-users are still unable to benefit from progress made in recent years. The most important aspect of CD-ROM technology is that it offers high-quality sound, surely the most important development in CALL over the last 20 years. One wonders how we did without it throughout the 70s and most of the 80s. CD-ROM, as opposed to CDI, points to the future. The medium is still finding its feet, however, and it is clear that program designers still have a lot to learn. In the meantime, I will conclude by presenting my own selection of CD-ROMs, which I consider to be good examples of the use of good pedagogy and appropriate use of CD-ROM technology:

TriplePlay Plus (Syracuse Language Systems) offers a game-like approach to language learning. As the title suggests, there are three levels of play, the first concentrating on words, the second on phrases, and the third on conversations. The quality of the sound output is excellent, and the learner can record his/her own voice, choosing different speeds of delivery by the native speaker There are text-based exercises too, e.g. the rearranging of jumbled sentences. The learner can choose to monitor his/her own playback or switch on the Automatic Speech Recognition software - which works quite well in this package. The topics covered are: Food, Numbers, People, Activities, Places & Transportation, Home & Office. The package is available in English, French, German, Spanish, Italian, Hebrew and Japanese.

Encounters (TELL Consortium, published by Hodder & Stoughton) is a series aimed at the adult beginner in French, German, Spanish, Italian or Portuguese. The approach is modular, functional and non-sequential. Each CD-ROM consists of 25 modules covering a variety of functions: e.g. Travel & Tourism, Asking for Directions, Introductions, etc. The student can participate in spoken dialogues, recording his/her own voice and matching it with the native speaker model. It is possible to explore each dialogue in more detail, seeking information on grammar, usage and cultural background. Optional exercises are also available.

The Tortoise and the Hare (Brøderbund) is one of the popular *Living Books*, most of which centre on a short story aimed at young children - although adults seem to find them just as entertaining. Aesop's fable of the race between the tortoise and the hare is presented here in a new light. Simon, the storytelling bird, acts as the narrator. The full text of the story appears on screen - in English or Spanish - and is first read out loud by a native speaker (American English or South American Spanish). The learner can click on any word in the text in order to hear it pronounced, but clicking on items in the pictures that illustrate the story brings a rich variety of surprises: chimney pots that wish one another "Good morning" or "Buenos dias", the politically correct tortoise that insists on newspapers being recycled, the rapping beaver - and many others.

The New Kid on the Block (Brøderbund) is another *Living Book*, but with a slightly different approach. Instead of dealing with just one story, this CD-ROM contains a series of amusing poems in English for young children, all of which have been written by Jack Prelutsky. The aim is to bring the poems to life. The learner can listen to the whole text of each poem and can then click on any word. A native speaker (American English) reads the individual word out loud and the meaning of the word is acted out in a series of animated cartoons. The animations are both memorable and humorous, proving that poetry can be fun.

All-in-One Language Fun (Syracuse Language Systems) offers an introduction to five foreign languages: French, German, Spanish, Japanese and English. The package is aimed at the younger learner (3-12) and concentrates entirely on listening skills through multimedia versions of familiar games: e.g. Jigsaw Puzzles, Memory Teasers, Simon Says, Bingo, Telling the Time, Dress the Child, etc. The package is full of illustrations, some of which are animated. The game in which the learner has to guide the mouse towards the cheese is particularly good for teaching prepositions of location and direction. Adults also seem to enjoy this CD-ROM.

En Route (Yorkshire Television & International Thompson) is aimed at secondary school learners of French. It is divided into ten comprehensive sections covering a wide range of everyday topics. Each section deals with a different topic and contains a variety of exercises. The package enables the user to record his/her own voice and compare it with a French native speaker. Students may also measure their progress via continuous assessment. There are hundreds of photographs, illustrations, video and audio clips, and online grammar help. Spanish and German companion CD-ROMs, entitled *En Marcha* and *Unterwegs*, are also available

Your Way (Syracuse Language Systems) is a multimedia CD-ROM consisting of a variety of branching conversations. Like Syracuse's other publication *TriplePlay Plus*, this package makes use of speech recognition - which again works quite well. The learner participates in conversations with more than one possible response and more than one outcome, so the conversations branch according to the learner's choices. It's an old idea but executed well in the context of this new medium. The conversations are complemented by a set of interactive games. The package includes a grammar reference section and bilingual glossary. Available in French and Spanish.

Who is Oscar Lake? (Language Publications Interactive) is similar in some respects to *Your Way*, the difference being that the learner is playing the key role in a mystery story. As the learner tries to solve the mystery he/she is confronted in the target language with an interesting cast of characters in real-world settings. The learner's mother tongue can be set to English, French, German, Italian or Spanish, making the software usable for a wide variety of different users. The video scenes run under QuickTime. They are a bit jerky but in the context of this CD-ROM they are a vital component for the interactive sequences: e.g. in one sequence the learner books a train ticket, hands the ticket clerk the money, picks up the ticket and puts it in a briefcase. The learner can choose to see the text of any conversation on screen, record his/her own voice, and see a translation.. The learner participates in the conversations by selecting alternative answers, so the conversation can develop in different ways - and so can the story. Over 1000 items of vocabulary are covered. All the learner has to do is click on any object in any scene, which causes a native speaker to pronounce the name of the object while the text appears on screen. Available in French, Spanish and English.

Cinemania (Microsoft Home) is included here partly because I am a film addict but also because I believe students should give careful thought to the films they choose to watch. This CD-ROM offers the user access to a selection of reference works containing reviews of thousands of films. The reviews are accompanied by biographies, still pictures, famous dialogues (together with transcriptions), musical excerpts and video clips. Yes, the motion video sequences are jerky, but how else does one convey the atmosphere of the remarkable tense scene in which Will Kane (Gary Cooper) waits for the vengeful Frank Miller (Ian MacDonald) to arrive on the 12 o'clock train in *High Noon*, and is there a better way of reminding oneself that Rick (Humphrey Bogart) did not say "Play it again, Sam" to Dooley Wilson in *Casablanca*? He actually said, "Sam, I thought I told you never to play..." before he caught sight of his lost love Ilsa (Ingrid Bergman) in his bar, the Café Americain: an unforgettable moment, captured in multimedia.

Encarta (Microsoft Home) is probably the best of the encyclopaedias on CD-ROM. *Encarta* is good example of a comprehensive hypertext system in which the user can browse at will. The text, audio, graphics and video clips are superb, and the user has access to an online dictionary, thesaurus, wordprocessor and atlas. In a recent browsing session, I started with *Wales*, which linked me to an article on the *Celtic Languages*. This took me to a selection of words and phrases in *Irish Gaelic*, which I was able to hear pronounced. Finally, I ended up in the section on *World Languages* and was able to compare ways of saying "Hello" in about 60 different languages, from Albanian to Zulu. I was also able to listen to Dylan Thomas reciting the opening lines of his poem *Do Not Go Gentle into That Good Night* and Robert Frost delivering *Fire and Ice*. The new version of *Encarta* has less of an American bias, and a French language version is in production.

The Grammar ROM (Longman) is aimed at learners of English as a Foreign Language. This is one of the few CD-ROMs I have seen that concentrate on grammar. All the key points of English grammar are covered: Verbs, Nouns and Articles, Modals, Conditionals The Passive, Adjectives and Adverbs, Questions, Prepositions, Clauses, Links, Reported Speech, Phrasal Verbs, Gerund and Infinitive. The learner can choose between English, French, German, Spanish and Italian as the language of on-screen instructions and spoken instructions. There is an online glossary and grammar reference section, accompanied by 300 exercises: e.g. multiple-choice and gap-filling exercises, comprehension exercises relating to written text and audio and video recordings, re-ordering of sentences, sequencing of activities. The CD-ROM includes lively cartoon drawings, authentic sound recordings, and motion video sequences taken from videos written by Ingrid Freebairn and Brian Abbs: *A Family Affair, Two Days in Summer, Face the Music*.

Longman Interactive English Dictionary (Longman) goes beyond the normal printed dictionary by offering the learner an extensive computer database consisting of text, sound, video clips and pictures. The *LIED* is based on printed versions of Longman's popular reference works for the student of English. As well as being able to read about grammar and meanings of words, the learner can hear how they are pronounced and see pictures and video clips that illustrate them. An impressive feature of this CD-ROM is the facility for linking the different reference works: e.g. it is possible to click on a word in the text of a transcript of a video sequence, look it up in order to check the meaning and then hear it pronounced in Received Pronunciation.

References

Coren, A. (1976) *The sanity inspector*, London: Hodder and Stoughton, Coronet Books Edition.

Davies, G. D. (1985) *Talking BASIC: an introduction to BASIC programming for users of language*, Eastbourne: Cassell.

Davies, G. D. (1991) "EXPODISC - an interactive videodisc package for learners of Spanish". In Savolainen, H. & Telenius, J. (eds.) *Eurocall 91: Proceedings*, Helsinki: Helsinki School of Economics: pp. 133-139.

Davies, G. D. (1992) "Computer assisted language learning". In Embleton, D.& Hagen, S. (eds.) *Languages and international business: a practical guide*, Sevenoaks: Hodder & Stoughton: pp. 112-123.

Davies, G. D. & Higgins, J. J. (1982) *Computers, language and language learning*, London: CILT.

Davies, G. D. & Higgins, J. J. (1985) *Using computers in language learning: a teacher's guide*, London: CILT.

Davies, G. D., Bangs, P. & Betts, F. (1994) *Investigation into the use of language training materials in SMEs with a special focus on those incorporating new technologies: study on Lingua Action III projects*, Brussels: Lingua Bureau, Commission of the European Communities. (Not generally available for public consultation.)

Davies, R. (1991) *ELNET Report: European Business and Languages Learning Network*, Southampton: CECOMM, Southampton Institute of Higher Education.

Davies, R. (1992) "ELNET: the European Learning Network". In Davies, G. D. & Hussey, M. (eds.) *New technology in language learning*, Frankfurt: Peter Lang Verlag: pp. 123-127.

Eastment, D. (1994) "CD-ROM: an overview of available materials", *Modern English Teacher* 3, 4: pp. 68-77.

Eastment, D. (1996) "The Internet for teachers and learners", *Modern English Teacher* 5, 2: pp. 58-82.

Ely, P. (1984) *Bring the lab back to life*, Oxford: Pergamon.

European Commission: Bureau Lingua/DELTA (1993) *Foreign language learning and the use of new technologies: conference proceedings*, Brussels: EC.

Garrett, N. "Where do we go from here - and who is leading the way?". In Savolainen, H. & Telenius, J. (eds.) *Eurocall 91: Proceedings*, Helsinki: Helsinki School of Economics: pp. 17-20.

Harnad, S. (1989) "Minds, Machines and Searle", *Journal of Experimental and Theoretical Artificial Intelligence* 1, 1.

Holmes, G. & Kidd, M. (1980) "The evolving case for computers in the study of modern languages", *ALLC Journal* 1, 1: pp. 8-10.

Johns, T. (1991) "Data-driven learning and the revival of grammar". In Savolainen, H. & Telenius, J. (eds.) *Eurocall 91: Proceedings*, Helsinki: Helsinki School of Economics: pp. 21-22.

Johns, T. & King, P. (eds.) (1991) *Classroom concordancing*, Special Issue of the *ELR Journal* 4, University of Birmingham: Centre for English Language Studies.

Jones, C. (1986) "It's not so much the program: more what you do with it: the importance of methodology in CALL", *System* 14, 2: pp. 171-178.

Last, R. W. (1989) *Artificial intelligence techniques in language learning.* Chichester: Ellis Horwood.

Laurillard, D. (1993) *Program design principles*, Hull: TELL Consortium, CTI Centre for Modern Languages, University of Hull.

Levy, M. (1996) *CALL: context and conceptualisation*, Oxford: Oxford University Press.

Otto, S. (1993) "Technology in academe: cautionary tales of where we should go and how we should get there". In Liddell, P. (ed.) *CALL: Theory and application. Proceedings of CCALL2/CCELAO2, the Second Canadian CALL Conference*, Victoria, Canada: University of Victoria.

Searle, J. R. (1980) "Minds, brains and programs", *Behavioural and Brain Sciences* 3: pp. 417-424.

Searle, J. R. (1982) "The Chinese Room revisited", *Behavioural and Brain Sciences* 5: pp. 345-348.

Tribble, C. & Jones, G. (1990) *Concordances in the classroom*, Harlow: Longman.

Turing, A. M. (1964) "Computing machinery and intelligence". In: Anderson, A. R. (ed.) *Minds and machines*, Engelwood Cliffs NJ: Prentice Hall.

Vilmi, R. (1996) "The HUT email writing project", *CALL Review*, (IATEFL SIG Newsletter) March Edition: pp. 8-9.

Willis, D. (1990) *The lexical syllabus*, London: Collins.

3. OLD TECHNOLOGY, NEW TECHNOLOGY: VIDEO MAKES A COME-BACK

Elspeth BROADY - United Kingdom

Video is no longer considered new technology in language teaching, yet one of the most exciting advances of the 1990's has been the integration of video into the panoply of media that can now be delivered by computer. The control and support of video input by computer - known as *interactive video* - has been possible for many years. Although its pedagogical potential was confirmed by early research (Watts, 1987), interactive video never achieved widespread up-take in language teaching, quite possibly because of the different standards developed for the laser disc technology delivering the video input (Kornum, 1992). The early interactive video systems, with bulky laser disc players and double screens - one for video input and one for computer commands - now appear curiously cumbersome next to the multimedia personal computer, where CD ROMs currently provide the standard storage technology for video input. Video can be displayed either in a window, along with windows displaying other types of information, or full-screen[1]. Interactive video may be 'dead' in its laser-disc form, but long live interactive multimedia!

This paper argues for a broad view of using video in language learning. It reviews existing approaches, focuses on some of the issues arising from the use of authentic TV, and tries to sketch the possibilities offered by multimedia video. Then, drawing on the work of an R & D project for the Council of Europe Workshop 9[2], it considers the value of video as a medium for learner production. The discussion throughout is situated within a changing methodological framework: if the 1980's were the decade of the 'communicative approach' and 'video', then the 1990's are the decade of learner

---

[1]   Currently, full-screen video of conventional VCR quality requires high level hardware and software, in particular an MPEG board. However, it is likely this will become standard in the near future.

[2]   I would like to acknowledge here the work of the R & D group on Using Video to Promote Oral Skills in Vocationally Oriented Language Learning. The project group consisted of Elspeth Broady; Galina Bondarchuk, Moscow Linguistic University; Maija Gulena, University of Latvia; Jean-Pierre Lemaire, Centre d'Autoformation, Huy, Belgium; Suliko Liiv, Tallin Pedagogical University; Birgit Lindström, Dragonskolan, Umeå, Sweden, and Zoltán Poór, Kecskemét College of Education, Hungary.
       Further contributions were made by Dominique Le Duc and Graham Townsend, University of Brighton Language Centre, and participants at Council of Europe Workshop 9B, in particular: Vasily Dublansky, Minsk, Belarus; Lidia Shashina, Volgograd Pedagogical University; Valentina Yepuri, Moldava State University; Stella Theocharous and Costas Markou, Ministry of Education, Cyprus.

independence and 'interactive multimedia'. The approach to technology underlying this discussion stresses what learners can do with it, not so much how it can 'instruct'.

3.1 The Consensus on Video

In 1990, Ian MacWilliam indicated thus the existence of a consensus on using video:

> "..there can be very few practising (and journal-reading) teachers with access to video who still need to be told that 'video places language in context' or who are as yet unaware of the virtues of the freeze-frame button." (MacWilliam, 1990: 157)

The potential for communicative language teaching of the *video mode* (that is, recordings of moving pictures with synchronous sound - the mode shared by video, film and television) is obvious. Of all media available to us, it provides the most accurate representation of language-in-use, that is, language embedded in a situation, used by speakers whose identity we 'read' from their physical appearance, and whose communicative intent is reinforced by a whole range of visually coded paralinguistic features[1]

If the call for a communicative approach to language teaching created enthusiasm for the video mode during the 1980s, it was the generalisation of new video technology (video tape, video cassette recorder/player, remote control) which enabled a principled video methodology to emerge. Other moving-picture, synchronous-sound delivery systems, such as film and broadcast TV, had been used in language teaching but their 'non-interruptable' quality limited the degree of active interaction possible. Their products were seen more as 'programmes' which replaced the teacher, rather than 'resources' to be exploited in interaction between teacher and learner, or by the learner him/herself (Allan, 1991: 59). The new video technology allowed recordings to be interrupted and used selectively; the two channels of sound and vision could easily be separated and the 'freeze-frame' button allowed for 'citation' and discussion of visual information, which could then be contextualised in the whole visual narrative. Viewing could become a far more active task, supporting a variety of exploitations.

The principle behind the established video methodology[2] is to use the medium to set up some kind of interpretation gap. This is done most typically by getting learners to interpret sound and pictures separately in silent viewing or sound-only activities. From the visual input, learners can be asked to predict what the video extract is about and the language which is likely to be used; from the audio input, learners can be asked to predict the contextual features of the language heard - for example, who is involved in

---

[1]   For in-depth discussion, see Willis (1983), Riley (1985) and Kellerman (1992).

[2]   Among the major contributors to the development of a video methodology have been: Lonergan (1984), Coste & Compte (1984), Allan (1985), Tomalin (1986), Hill (1989) and Stempleski & Tomalin (1990).

the exchange? where does it take place? Such speculation is then followed by bi-modal viewing, during which learners compare their interpretations with the original.

This approach has a four-fold rationale:

1. it provides learners with, or invites learners to find, a *context for interpretation* of linguistic input, thus focusing their comprehension;

2. in so doing, it promotes *comprehension strategies*, that of using visual information - more accessible than linguistic input - to guess at what is being said; or, in the case of interpreting aural linguistic information only, that of visualising a communicative situation in which linguistic input makes sense;

3. because of the 'interpretation gap' (sound-only or pictures-only versions of a video are necessarily ambiguous) learners have a *motivation to communicate* with each other and with their teacher;

4. when they come to bi-modal viewing, they have a *purpose for viewing*, i.e. they need to compare their predictions with the original audio-visual message. In this way, the task encourages learners to practise their comprehension skills in a focused, and arguably more natural, way.

3.2 Exploiting Authentic Television

The consensus methodology identified above applies generally to exploitation of any video recording. A particularly rich and varied source of video input for language learning is provided by target language television, now directly available to many language learners in Europe, thanks to satellite and cable transmission. In line with Krashen's (1985) call for language learning to be focused around large quantities of meaningful and motivating input, and the importance placed by the communicative approach on 'authenticity'[1] - that is, materials designed to have a real communicative function, usually aiming at native speakers rather than language learners - there has been much enthusiasm for exploiting this resource (Coleman, 1990; Higham, 1993).

However, it is easy to forget that what foreign language channels in fact provide are TV programmes whose primary aim is not to contextualise language for language learners, but to amuse, inform, persuade and generally represent - to themselves - members of a particular culture. The foreign language learner often does not share the background knowledge - we can refer to it as *'cultural knowledge'* - needed to interpret them. A news report on a cycling demonstration in Paris from the French channel TF1 offers an obvious example. The journalist's report begins:

---

[1]   For discussion of 'authenticity' see McDonough & Shaw, 1993: Chapter 3 and Kramsch, 1993: Chapter 6.

"Nous sommes en 1993 après Jésus Christ. Toute la Gaule est occupée par les voitures. Toute? Non, un petit groupe de cyclistes résiste toujours victorieusement à l'envahisseur motorisé."

(TF1, Journal de 20h, 5/6/93 reproduced in Broady & Meinhof, 1995: 79)

Presumably most of TF1's audience recognised the reporter's 'borrowing' of the introduction to the *Astérix* cartoon books, and interpreted this as lending a gently ironic tone to the report, very much in keeping with the high spirits of the demonstrators depicted later. But how does a non-French viewer interpret this commentary, especially when it is presented over negative black and white pictures of a traffic jam, then an exhaust pipe, then - coinciding with the words "un petit groupe" - colour footage of a rather large gathering of cyclists in one of Paris' main squares! The pictures in no way support interpretation of the verbal input, except perhaps if the learner is televisually sophisticated enough to recognise that the shift to negative black and white must imply a break with 'normal' information-focused reporting conventions. Even so, without the background knowledge that would allow the connection with Astérix, the first six seconds of this report are likely to remain totally opaque to the average non-native viewer. Such problems clearly arise when learners work with authentic press articles, but the demands of on-line listening can exacerbate them, since not even the basic linguistic reference can be established. This brief example makes the paradox of authentic television clear. Because it conveys 'real' language used by 'real' people in a 'real' situation, it is generally perceived as motivating and interesting by learners. Yet this very cultural authenticity can render it frustratingly obscure. But is this a 'real' problem?

3.3 Schema as Viewing Strategies

Non-native viewers are not the only ones whose understanding is impaired when pictures and commentary do not correspond closely: it happens to native viewers too (Grimes, 1990). Further, not all francophone viewers will necessarily share the knowledge assumed by, say, TF1 reporters and producers. What native viewers do when faced with ambiguous televisual information is extract what makes sense to them and ignore the rest. The problem for non-native speakers is they often lack the confidence to do this and assume that they need to understand every word. With such a strategy, the riches of authentic television are likely to remain buried. For this reason, a number of practitioners have advocated helping learners develop *'viewing strategies'*, in particular, mobilising their existing knowledge or *'schema'* in order to provide an instant framework for initial interpretation[1]. Schema can refer to content (e.g. learners watching a TV report about the ozone layer need to ask themselves: what do I know already know about the ozone layer? what are the issues likely to be raised? with what connections between them?), but also televisual genres, which appear to be characterised

---

[1]   Altman (1990) offers a useful introduction to the role of schema theory in exploiting video in general, not just authentic TV.

by fairly generalisable information structures (Meinhof, 1990 and personal communication). Meinhof & Bergman (1993), for example, suggest non-native viewers of news broadcasts focus first on "pattern questions" which can generally be applied to any exemplar of a particular news genre. For instance, the pattern questions they propose for environmental reports are "Which aspect of the environment is affected? Can the causes of the problems be identified? What would be required to solve the problems? Is it likely that the problems will be solved?" (*op.cit*: 43). Meanwhile, Tudor & Tuffs (1991) show how learners' activation of either a content schema and a formal schema (that is, awareness of the typical rhetorical patterns that reoccur in the organisation of information, such as chronological sequence or a problem-solution model) can enhance comprehension of TV documentary material. If learners can activate these various types of schema, then they should be able to approach authentic TV with greater confidence, focusing their attention first on identifying the extent to which the broadcast confirms their existing schema and second, on identifying the new and unpredicted information.

3.4 Cultural Knowledge and Cultural Differences - a Puzzle not a Problem

Given the importance of *cultural awareness* in developing communicative competence in a foreign language (Byram & Morgan, 1994), it seems vital to encourage learners not to ignore assumed cultural knowledge, but rather see it as a puzzle to be investigated. Esch and King (1993) suggest learners list cultural references after initial viewing and then explore their meaning through dictionaries and encyclopaediae, as well as complementary press and radio reports. In response to the specific example from TF1 quoted above, Broady & Meinhof (1995: 59) provide learners with a copy of the introduction to *Astérix le Gaulois* and invite them to interpret the connection. Watching authentic TV, then, should not be reduced to a mere linguistic decoding exercise: with its complex cultural resonances[1] it offers a much richer, and more challenging, resource which should stimulate further work with target language materials.

Claire Kramsch states:

> "The issue that is raised by the use of real-life materials is that culture is a reality that is social, political and ideological and that the difficulty of understanding cultural codes stems from the difficulty of viewing the world from another perspective, not of grasping another lexical or grammatical code." (Kramsch, 1993: 188)

While, as indicated earlier, it may be useful for learners to be made aware of universal patterns in televisual material, it is also important to sensitise them to the different perspective" on the world offered by authentic TV. This may quite simply involve inviting learners to contrast what they see on target language television with what they are familiar with from their L1 television, either in terms of images (e.g. Does a French pop festival, as reported on TV, look like a British one? Does the French Chambre des

---

[1]   See Tudor (1987) and Kramsch (1993), Chapter 6, for more extensive discussion.

Députés look like the British House of Commons?) or in terms of the broadcast itself (What differences are there in the way different national channels report the same news event?). Cultural awareness is about observing, exploring and understanding a different organisation of reality and images no doubt offer a more immediate stimulus to this than printed text. The video mode has the advantage (or disadvantage!) of appearing to simulate experience: with its strong affective impact, it can thus offer very powerful input to developing cultural awareness within a learning environment[1]. (We discuss later how video production work can enhance encounters with the target language culture.)

3.5 Learning to View and Viewing to Learn

In the preceding paragraph, recordings from authentic TV were presented as cultural artefacts to be explored and analysed. Watching television for native speakers, however, is usually an *on-line activity*, one which is rarely replicated in classrooms in its "real operating conditions" (Johnson, 1996: 122). Dieuzeide (1991) argues that it should be:

> ".. seul le direct (*live use*) rapproche des conditions de la situation linguistique véritable, face à un flux de communication linéaire, irréversible et non maîtrisable, qui contraint à mobiliser en même temps tous les mécanismes de détection et d'inférence". (Dieuzeide, 1991: 17)

Using live broadcasts in the language classroom forces learners to use guess-work strategies, to focus - like native speakers - *not* on what they *don't* understand, but on what they *do*, since they will not have the chance to replay or pause. This type of approach has the further advantage of not involving teachers in extensive preparation. It focuses on the skill of viewing, and may be referred to as '*learning to view*'. Training confidence in this skill should encourage learners to adopt target language viewing habits outside the classroom, alongside their L1 viewing.

In contrast, Vanderplank (1990: 222) seems to be advocating a '*viewing to learn*' approach. He argues that the value of authentic TV as a *language resource* has been neglected in favour of "using television to activate language already in the learners' heads". He seeks to redress the balance by advocating the use of video recordings with *sub-titles*. The idea is not simply to help learners understand broadcasts at gist level, but to enrich their linguistic intake. His research (Vanderplank, 1988) found that a combination of providing subtitles and setting basic tasks did encourage learners to 'take out' language from the programmes and use it in their own production. Rather than making the viewing experience less authentic, Vanderplank claims that subtitles make it more authentic for non-native speakers because they are able to view programmes with a greater degree of linguistic confidence and can thus appreciate them in a way that more closely resembles that of a native speaker.

---

[1]   Tomalin & Stempleski (1993) offer a wealth of ideas on promoting cultural awareness, many of which exploit video input.

Extensive research (Vanderplank, 1988; Garza, 1991; Danan, 1992; Borrás & Lafayette, 1994) supports the use of sub-titling to enhance comprehension and retention of L2 audio-visual information; in particular, it confirms the value of bi-modal subtitling (L2 audio + L2 sub-titles) and less predictably, reverse sub-titling, that is L2 sub-titles over L1 audio. Research conducted in North America (Danan, 1992) suggests that standard L1 sub-titling hinders, rather than helps, retention of L2 language items, although Dutch research in Holland found that viewers did pay attention to the L2 audio track of news presentations sub-titled in L1, which would suggest that regular exposure to L2 video input, even if sub-titled in L1, could lead to incidental target language learning, or at least target language maintenance (de Bot et al., 1986).

So far, we have discussed the rationale behind consensus video methodology and have looked at some of the issues relating to the exploitation of authentic TV. In both cases, it is usually assumed that the video/TV material will be exploited *collectively* in a classroom with one video screen, one teacher and many learners. In such a setting, it makes perfect sense to place the emphasis on interpretation gap and using video - with much of the focus on the images - as a stimulus for discussion (what Vanderplank referred to as "language already in learners' heads"). Video recordings delivered by a single VCR in the corner of the classroom controlled by the teacher are probably a less than effective medium for focusing attention on specific exemplars of language use[1]. As Vanderplank (1993: 11) has noted:

"...controlling sound is inherently difficult. You cannot freeze sound, only replay it and replaying segments of videotape can be awkward (...) unless and until some simple means of controlling the verbal element without massive teacher preparation and intervention becomes widely and inexpensively available, teachers will feel they have little choice but to concentrate on the visual element."

Print is clearly the best mode for "controlling the verbal element", but apart from on-screen sub-titles, using the print mode simultaneously with video is notoriously problematic; even if teachers have the time to prepare worksheets, many will have had the disappointing experience of seeing their learners focus exclusively on the worksheet and ignore the video screen. However, with video now integrated into computer-based multimedia - or perhaps better, hypermedia - the limitations imposed by conventional video technology no longer have to apply.

3.6 Digital Video, Multimedia and Hypermedia

Hypermedia refers to the possibilities offered by multimedia computers of simultaneous and interlinking access to any number of text, graphics, audio, photo and video files.

---

[1]   This point appears to be confirmed by American research (Secules, Herron & Tomasello, 1992) which found that students taking an experimental course based around video input failed to show any comparative advantage on learning of specific linguistic structures when compared with a control group in a direct method class, while there was an effect on listening comprehension skills.

This kind of functionality removes the problem referred to above of combining video with other media: all information can be presented on the same screen. Digital video offers us much *greater control*; access is no longer linear, individual frames can easily be selected and manipulated, fine segments of language can be identified and replayed. In this way, digital video starts to have some of the "freezing" qualities of print which make it so useful a medium for detailed reflection on language. The visual information can also be 'frozen' and examined in far greater detail than was possible with video delivered through a VCR. These possibilities are only just beginning to be explored[1].

We have seen above some quite different emphases in exploiting video input - from focus on visuals as a support for comprehension and discussion, to viewing schema, direct viewing, cultural codes and language. While different teachers may favour different approaches, there is little to say that a particular approach is at all times inappropriate. Different skills are being trained, and different insights triggered by the different types of exercises, and they are not necessarily exclusive. What we have termed the 'learning to view' approach, which emphasises the skill of global comprehension, can be followed by 'viewing to learn' with more detailed exploration of the cultural issues raised in the material, and closer attention on the language used.

What a multimedia computer can provide is simultaneous access to any of these various exercises, plus all kinds of support materials. For example, different types of sub-titles and transcripts can be made available, with hypertext links to glossaries and files of information which, for instance, might shed light on cultural references such as the *Astérix* problem discussed earlier. The first advantage of multimedia video is that learners themselves can easily select the level of *language support* they need in order to get from the video materials what they require. Brett (1995, 81) describes the principle, as illustrated in the University of Wolverhampton's multimedia package *English for Business*.:

> "The language input in this multimedia package can be delivered through, and made more or less accessible by, learner-selected use of any of the following different combinations of media: audio, audio with subtitles; audio, subtitles and graded, sequenced tasks; video, video with subtitles; or video, subtitles and graded sequenced task. (...)The strong claim is that the language input provided by the various, learner-selected, combinations of media, is input that can be more finely tuned and therefore, is such that it may be more readily converted to 'intake'".

Secondly, learners can access via one technology *any number of sources* which allow them to interpret, say, a cultural issue, more widely and deeply. Kramsch (1993: 199) offers a vision of multimedia's potential for presenting learners with multiple viewpoints on regionalism in Brittany.

---

[1]   Only a minority of CD-ROM multimedia packages for language learning appearing in the UK-based *Camsoft Directory* currently contain full moving picture video.

"Instead of plowing through dense newspaper articles packed with unknown words and facts, or even viewing television broadcasts spoken at top speed and taken out of their sociocultural context, you are about to take a video adventure. .. On one screen, an animated film introduces Monsieur Dupont, who invites you into his office in a small town in Brittany. (...) on the other screen, a colour film shows Brittany farmers dumping truck loads of artichokes on the roads. On the first screen, Monsieur Dupont, the préfet, confides that the farmers are discontent and he needs you to help find the reason. The evidence is in his notebooks and cabinets, on the screen in front of you. (..) you open a file cabinet, take out a folder marked 'Interviews'... the screen fills with the image of a real farmer, talking about the prices of artichokes, the eating habits of the French and complaining about the central government. The file cabinet turns out to contain a dozen similar interviews (...) along with animated maps and articles about regionalism (...) You also have access to endless vocabulary dictionaries, transcriptions, subtitles and so on. Using the mouse, you browse through the films, text, and photographs, letting your curiosity lead the way"

A third example of the potential of multimedia video is the *interactive video narrative*, probably best exemplified by *A la rencontre de Philippe* (Murray et al., 1989), developed in the United States. Here, video's capacity to simulate experience is enhanced by inviting the learner at various stages to influence the story by making choices based on his/her understanding of the issues. The video story offers a contextualisation - and motivation - for practising a variety of language skills, as learners may access other inputs - texts, audio recordings - to help them make their decision.

In these examples, we see how video's strength in contextualising language-in-use and simulating experience can be enhanced by the addition of other media and increased interactivity for the learner. Just as we start to glimpse the possibilities, the technological framework for delivery of multimedia/hypermedia video is changing. Video can now be accessed with increasing ease via the Internet, thus obviating the need for CD-ROM as a portability device. With this explosion in opportunities for audio-visual communication, our reflection on how we exploit video for language learning needs to be sharpened, bearing in mind the following points:

i.   we are now dealing not with video alone, but *integrated* with other media;
ii.   video is not just input for 'collective' comprehension, but input which can be finely manipulated and interacted with by *individuals or small groups* based at personal computers;
iii.   video is no longer just a 'resource', but also a medium of *interactive communication.*

3.7 Video as a Productive Medium

This leads us to consider the value of video as a medium for learner production. Over the last decade, video cameras have increased in portability and decreased in price and a growing literature attests to their usefulness in language learning[1]. Video editing can now be undertaken on a computer in a similar way to the manipulation of text and graphic information in word-processing.[2] Just as word-processing (now desk-top publishing!) can motivate written expression, so desk-top video editing will no doubt stimulate greater productive use of video within education. The likelihood of this is all the greater, now that digital video files can be transmitted electronically.

As with video play-back, a methodology has been built up for exploiting video production in language learning[3]. Two types of video recording task are distinguished: video feedback, where learners are filmed in some kind of communicative performance, such as a simulation or a presentation, and the video record is then used to support detailed feed-back, and *video project work*, where video is used as a medium for student productions, such as documentaries, simulated promotional videos and news items.

Video feed-back has been a conventional use of video in both language teaching and professional skills training, but many language teachers are aware of the difficulties in exploiting it effectively. Firstly, learners are understandably uncomfortable to watch their performance if the focus is on its imperfections. Secondly, the density of information which video provides, coupled with its sequential nature, can make teacher-led video feed-back a long, drawn-out process. Cooper et al. (1991: 5) in a key book on video production explicitly distance themselves from this type of activity. The Video R & D Group, however, found that video feed-back could be useful, in particular to help learners develop self and peer assessment skills. This required careful framing of the post-viewing tasks, with feed-back grids focusing learners' attention away from detailed error correction of individuals - at least in the first instance - and onto more global and collective aspects of performance such as how effectively roles had been created or whether a group had acted with formality appropriate to the situation. In the case of a conference simulation[4], for example, learners were invited to focus on the way in which members of the group recorded managed turn-taking and interruptions. This emphasis on the wider communicative situation, rather than on linguistic failings, also meant that students started to pay much greater attention to the kinesic features of

---

[1]   For recent contributions, see Coleman, 1992; Savage, 1994; Poór, 1994; Broady & Le Duc, 1995 and Gardner, 1995.

[2]   Desk-top video editing currently requires high-level hardware and software in order to compress the huge video storage files, but, given consumer interest, it can only be a matter of time before desktop video editing is widely and cheaply available.

[3]   Key contributions include Geddes & Sturtridge, 1982; Lonergan, 1984; Allan, 1985 and Lonergan, 1990. Much of what follows here draws on the work of the Video R&D group from Workshop 9. The group's work is reported as a collection of case studies: *Focus on the Learner: Using the Video Camera in Vocationally Oriented Language Learning*, available from Elspeth Broady, University of Brighton Language Centre, Brighton BN1 9PH.

[4]   Reported by Birgit Lindström for Workshop 9.

communication - such as eye contact and body language - often ignored by teachers and students alike[1].

A further finding of the project group was that as video recordings were repeated and integrated into a cycle of activities, so learners became increasingly confident in performing in front of a video camera and more comfortable with evaluating their own and other's performances. Learners need to be given opportunities to put into practice what they have learned from watching a first performance and have the satisfaction of seeing their improvement. In this way, video recording can provide a powerful stimulus for learners to become involved in self and peer-assessment. Students in several of the groups studied were aware that video recording could be intimidating, but at the same time, acknowledged its value in making them think more deeply about their own communication skills.

3.8 Video Project Work

As video has become more familiar as a productive medium, so video project work has gained ground. This involves learners using video as a *creative medium* and all practitioners attest to its motivating nature. Learners feel that they are doing something 'real' with the target language when, for example, they produce a documentary about their education system for teachers from their partner school or even a simple scenario they have written: they are using the target language to produce something which is meaningful to them[2]. The video product itself is in fact only a small part of a wider pedagogic task, which can involve a wide variety of target language skills as learners research and prepare for their video. The particular technology of the video camera is not fundamental - project work can lead to outcomes in other media - but video seems to generate strong motivation in learners and encourages focused work on oral communication skills, as well as offering opportunities for integrating linguistic with non-linguistic means of communication (moving images, still images, graphics, music etc.) - particularly useful for involving less confident students.

The video camera can be a particularly valuable tool in facilitating 'encounter projects' (Legutke & Thomas, 1991: 161) which bring learners into purposeful contact with members of the target language culture. For example, French and English students at Liverpool John Moores University and Université de Paris-Sorbonne[3] work together to make documentaries about local firms, based on interviews filmed within the company. This task brings them into contact with staff at all levels, exposes them directly to

---

[1]   Kellerman (1992) calls for greater attention to this area.

[2]   These two ideas for using video were developed respectively by Zoltán Poór and Dominique Le Duc.

[3]   Reported by Graham Townsend for Workshop 9. See also Townsend, 1993.

issues of corporate concern and sensitises them to the types of communication skills required in business.

Further, video projects engage not just language skills but organisational skills too, for project groups have to define their purpose, allocate roles, select relevant documentation, and prepare their content effectively for the video medium. While a written text can be - in fact invariably is - produced by an individual, a video project by definition requires group co-operation and management. Even if these cannot be considered *language* skills, they are important skills for learning and for life.

A key concern for Video R & D group was the *post-viewing stage* of video projects. Detailed linguistic error correction would again seem to be inappropriate: since much of the detailed language work involved should take place before the video recording is made, error correction would seem most appropriate as learners prepare drafts of their material. The conclusion was that post-viewing assessment of video projects should focus either on the communicative intent of the video (e.g. how effective a documentary is this? would it get its message across effectively to the intended audience?) or on the learning experience (e.g. what do you feel worked well in your video? what would you change if you had the chance to do it again? what do you feel you have learned in the process?). Again this more wide ranging evaluation ensured that learners did not feel their linguistic weaknesses had been exposed, but were nevertheless encouraged to reflect explicitly on their own work and its value.

3.9 A Task-Based Framework

Both the productive uses of video discussed above can be seen as fitting in with an approach which sees learning as organised around a *task*, such as making a video or performing a role play (Legutke & Thomas, 1991). Once the key task has been identified, the learning which needs to take place 'upstream' in preparation can be planned, and the focus for evaluation 'downstream' can be decided. As indicated in the model below, the cycle of learning activities thus falls into three stages: preparation/planning, presentation or performance of the task, and evaluation. In this way, different learning activities are motivated by the target task: learners should perceive their learning as 'going somewhere', as well as 'relating back' to previous activities. Fundamental to this view is that learners learn through doing things and then reflecting on the *process*, as well as on the product of their efforts. Fundamental too is that learners themselves manage the realisation of their task, with the teacher acting as a manager of resources and a guide.

A TASK-BASED FRAMEWORK (Based on Legutke & Thomas, 1991: 169-181)

PREPARATION
   Task introduction
   Learners are introduced to the task and working groups are formed

   Topic discussion
   Learners discuss their initial ideas on the topic

Research and Data collection
Learners define who does what and gather necessary material needed to perform the task

Organising material for presentation
Learners decide how they are going to present their material
TASK PRESENTATION
Learners complete and present their task in a particular medium

EVALUATION
Product Evaluation
The presentation is reviewed

Process Evaluation
The organisation of work leading to the presentation is reviewed

Objectives for further work
Learners take stock and decide what they need to do next

Conclusion

In this article, we have charted some of the ways in which video has been used in language teaching and some of the new possibilities offered by recent technological advances. One of the general consequences of the so-called 'information revolution' is that teachers and learners are faced with a far wider range of *tools and resources* for language learning than ever before: satellite and cable TV, multimedia information accessible via the Internet, desk-top publishing, desk-top video, e-mail and video conferencing. But many of these resources are not carefully organised for language learners and teachers: they are 'raw' materials or 'raw' opportunities for learning. In other words, for learning to take place, it is not enough for them to be available; they need to be exploited in purposeful ways. Teachers need to define tasks that will motivate learners to use these resources, as well as ways to help them reflect on what they are learning, and how to organise and maintain that knowledge and skill independently. The key question is probably less how teachers exploit this diversity, but how teachers help learners to exploit it. This means helping learners develop the confidence to work with material that is not immediately comprehensible and may not meet their immediate needs. This presupposes that learners learn to define their needs and select resources accordingly. It further presupposes that they learn to monitor the effectiveness of their learning and adapt their learning strategies if necessary. All of these skills associated with what is generally referred to as learner autonomy are now as vital to language learners as the conventional 'language knowledge' of grammar and vocabulary. The task-based framework presented above acknowledges this and provides a framework for promoting both language and learning skills. Within this framework, technology provides tools and resources, but it is the learner who remains firmly at the centre.

References

Allan, M. (1985, reprinted in 1991) *Teaching English with Video*. Longman.

Altman, R. (1990) "Towards a new video pedagogy: the role of schema theory and discourse analysis" *IALL Journal of Language Learning Technologies* 23/1: pp. 9-16.

Borrás, I. & Lafayette, R. (1994) "Effects of multimedia courseware subtitling on speaking performance of college students" *Modern Language Journal* 78/1 pp. 61-75.

Brett, P. (1995) "Multimedia for listening comprehension: the design of a multimedia-based resource for developing listening skills" *System* 23/1: pp. 77-85.

Broady, E. & Le Duc, D. (1995) "Learner autonomy and the video camera: a wider role for video recording activities?" *Language Learning Journal* 11: pp. 74-77.

Broady, E. & Meinhof, U. (1995) *Télé-textes* Activity Book, Video and CD-ROM. Oxford University Press.

Byram, M. & Morgan, C. and colleagues (1994) *Teaching-and-Learning Language-and-Culture*. Multilingual Matters.

Coleman, J.A. (1990) "Starting with satellite: a basic guide to using off-air video recordings in the language classroom" *Language Learning Journal* 2.

Coleman, J.A. (1992) "Project-based learning, transferable skills, information technology and video" *Language Learning Journal* 5: pp. 35-37.

Cooper, R., Lavery, M. & Rinvolucri, M. (1991) *Video*. Oxford University Press.

Coste, D. & Compte, C. (1984) "Des vidéos dans la classe: interactivité et choix méthodologiques" *Die Neueren Sprachen* 83/3: pp. 259-275.

Danan, M. (1992) "Reversed sub-titling and dual coding theory: new directions for foreign language instruction" *Language Learning* 42/4: pp. 497-527.

de Bot, K., Jagt, J., Jenssen, H., Kessels, E. & Schils, E. (1986) "Foreign language TV and language maintenance" *Second Language Research* 2: pp. 72-82.

Dieuzeide, Henri (1991) "L'utilisation des images reçues par satellite: une problématique pour l'enseignement des langues vivantes" Animator's Text, Workshop 7A "Using information and communication technology in modern language teaching and learning in Europe" Council of Europe, 26 November 1991.

Esch, E. & King, A. (1993) "Monsieur Dumas, qui c'est? Documents authentiques et appropriation du role de destinataire par les apprenants" *Mélanges CRAPEL* 21: pp. 83-97.

Garza, T. (1991) "Evaluating the use of captioned video materials in advanced language learning" *Foreign Language Annals* 24/3: pp. 239-258.

Geddes, M. & Sturtridge, G. (1982) *Video in the Language Classroom*. Heinemann.

Grimes, T. (1990) "Audio-video correspondence and its role in attention and memory" *Educational Technology Research and Development* 38:pp. 15-25.

Gardner, D. (1995) "Student produced video documentary provides a real reason for using the target language" *Language Learning Journal* 12: pp. 54-56.

Higham, J. (1993) *Direct Broadcasting by Satellite*. Report for Welsh Office Satellites in Schools Initiative, National Council for Educational Technology.

Hill, B. (1989) *Making the Most of Video*. CILT, London.

Johnson, K. (1996) *Language Teaching and Skill Learning*. Blackwell.

Kellerman, S. (1992) "I see what you mean: the role of kinesic behaviour in listening and implications for foreign and second language learning" *Applied Linguistics* 13/3: pp. 239-258.

Kornum, L (1990) "Interactive Video in Denmark" *Language Learning Journal* 1: pp. 52-54.

Kramsch, C. (1993) *Context and Culture in Language Teaching*. Oxford University Press.

Krashen, S. (1985) *The Input Hypothesis*. Longman.

Legutke, M. & Thomas, H. (1991) *Process and Experience in the Language Classroom.*. Longman.

Lonergan, J. (1984) *Video in Language Teaching*. Cambridge University Press.

Lonergan, J. (1990) *Making the Most of Your Video Camera*. CILT, London.

MacWilliam, I. (1990) "Video and language comprehension" in Rossner, R. & Bolitho, R. (eds.) *Currents of Change in English Language Teaching*. Oxford University Press.

McDonough, J. & Shaw, C. (1993) *Materials and Methods in ELT*. Blackwell.

Meinhof, U. (1990) "Verständnisstrategien für fremdsprachige Fernsehnachricten" *Die Neueren Sprachen* 89/6

Meinhof, U. & Bergman, M. (1993) *ITN World News*. Activity Book and Video. Oxford University Press.

Murray, J., Morgenstern, D. & Furstenberg, G. (1989) "The Athena Language-Learning Project: design issues for the next generation of computer-based language-learning tools" in Smith, W.F. (ed.) *Modern Technology in Foreign Language Education: Applications and Projects*. National Textbook Company.

Poór, Zoltán (1994) *A videotechnika produktív alkalmazása az általános iskolai nyelvoktatásban*. Ph.D. thesis. Kecskemét, Hungary.

Riley, P. (1985) "Viewing comprehension: l'oeil écoute" in Riley, P. (ed.) *Discourse and Learning*. Longman.

Savage, W. (1994) "Learner-directed video" in Jung, H. & Vanderplank, R. (eds.) *Barriers and Bridges: Media Technology in Language Learning*. Peter Lang.

Secules, T., Herron, C. & Tomasello, M. (1992) "The effect of video context on foreign language learning" *The Modern Language Journal* 76/4: pp. 480-490.

Stempleski, S. & Tomalin, B. (1990) *Video in Action*. Prentice-Hall International.

Tomalin, B. (1986) *Video, TV and Radio in the English Class*. Macmillan.

Tomalin, B. & Stempleski, S. (1993) *Cultural Awareness*. Oxford University Press.

Townsend, G. (1993) "Learning through videoed interviews in companies, with a little help from Jean-Paul Sartre, Peter Barkworth and the 'Image Manipulators' " in *Multimédia Transmanche* 5: 109-122. Centre d'Histoire des Idées dans les Iles Britanniques, Actes du Colloque du 20 mars, 1993, Presses de l'Université de Paris-Sorbonne.

Tudor, I. (1987) "Video as a means of cultural familiarization" *System*, 15: pp. 203-207.

Tudor, I. & Tuffs, R. (1991) "Formal and content schema activation in L2 viewing comprehension" *RELC Journal*, December, 1991.

Vanderplank, R. (1988) "The value of teletext subtitles for language learning" *English Language Teaching Journal.* 42: pp. 272-281.

Vanderplank, R. (1990) "Paying attention to the words: practical and theoretical problems in watching television programmes with uni-lingual (CEEFAX) subtitles" *System*, 18/2: pp. 221-234.

Vanderplank, R. (1993) "A very verbal medium: language learning through closed captions" *TESOL Journal*, 3/1: pp. 10-14

Watts, C.J. (1987) *The Use of Interactive Video in Language Learning* Unpublished M.Phil. Thesis, University of Brighton Language Centre.

Willis, J. (1983) "The role of the visual element in spoken discourse: implications for the exploitation of video in the EFL classroom" in McGovern, J. (ed.) *Video Applications in English Language Teaching*. Pergamon Press, in association with the British Council.

4. A PEDAGOGY OF THE HYPERMEDIA

Bernard MORO - France

The current educational background is favourable to new technologies

Looking back to December 1991 and the opening of Council of Europe Workshop 7A in Paris, I realise that it coincided in time with two events apparently light years from each other. One was the very beginning of hypertext software that could be used as authoring programs for didactic purposes. Another was that European governments were implementing very democratic educational policies, keeping young people as long as possible within educational structures, in an attempt both to meet the requirements of the job market for better-skilled workers, and to push down unemployment statistics.

In France for example, the goal for several years now has been to get 80% of the secondary school population over the hurdle of the *Baccalauréat*. This implies that from say 2nd- to 10th-graders there is virtually no selection, and that parents can always demand that their children move up to the next grade, whatever the advice of the staff.

Whether this is a satisfactory approach for the efficiency of future generations is not a question to be debated here. But the heart of the matter is for us to see how we, teachers of the near-21st century, can cope with our mission, given this environment.

One solution is pedagogical differentiation, whereby students are made conscious of their specific assets and needs, and teachers react at classroom level by devising activities targeted to the various requirements involved. Another is to expose learners to a self-learning environment based on IT, where there is no peer or teacher pressure; where they can learn at their own pace. It is our role to design, or to define the agenda for, applications that will be sufficiently profound, varied and visual for every profile of learner to be stimulated and progress.

Non-textual information plays a specific role in the hypermedia

Whether as designers or users, if we are to take part in the exposure of learners to didactic environments based on hypermedia, we must understand what their original cognitive aspects were.

Most of us have a reasonably accurate analysis of how textual information is understood by the reader, but we are far less aware of how visual and sound objects are captured and processed by the subject. We should be able to apprehend both their evident and hidden contents. The essential interface of the computer with its human partner is the screen. It is a visual surface. Its composition is not innocent, it obeys rules and conventions that have always existed in creating images, and it elicits from the viewer specific responses, of which we must be aware.

A few guidelines on visual conventions may prove useful

- An "X" composition, or perpendicular lines, as well as symmetries and vast perspectives, will give a sense of stability, order, peace and harmony, while on the contrary an absence of lines and contours will convey anxiety and chaos.

- A visual is a surface. The bigger an element, compared with others within the visual space of the picture, the more importance it has in the eyes of the author.

- A very high horizon encloses the viewer and deliberately creates a claustrophobic impression, while a low horizon leaves him a lot of freedom.

- A high-angle shot - or downward shot - whereby the viewer is made to look down on the subject, is obviously ironical. Conversely, the upward shot makes the subject more impressive, sometimes even threatening.

- Left-right dynamics refer to the well-established convention that the right of the picture represents its future, while the left part stands for its past. A sensation of left-right movement will therefore connote progress. This is true for most pictures, except in the United States with those images related to the myth of the Old West, in which for obvious reasons the right part symbolises the East, while the left represents the West, the Frontier - progress.

- Finally, a fair amount of images are allusions to well-known icons, and the message is the result of the deviation between the actual picture the viewer is looking at and the reference he has kept in his mind. The *Mona Lisa* is one such example, which has been tampered with into innumerable versions. It has been tested that people with no specific training were able to identify her even when 90% of the visual information had been filtered out. Michelangelo's *Hand of God* has had a similar fate...

Of children and Scriptures

Beyond this complex use of visual information lies a far more challenging aspect of the hypermedia software technology. It stems from their very structure, and will probably change not only the status of documents as we know them, but also our modes of access to information in general.

Watch a child move about in a kindergarten playground. His moves are unpredictable. His steps lead him to where his curiosity is attracted. Now his curiosity works along associative thought patterns. One stimulus generates an idea, which calls for verification, which in turn generates another idea, and so forth. The experimental process whereby the child gets in touch with his environment is therefore absolutely random, and this is what allows him to absorb the most, to maximise learning while minimising acquisition time. Random access to knowledge - or direct access, as I.T. terminology goes - seems to be an inborn and natural mode, and very likely the most effective, too.

Now watch adults move along in, say, an art gallery. Their moves are totally predictable, as if they were following a track, which is probably the case since the exhibit has to be sequentially organised for sheer practical reasons. Besides, adults will always tend to look for some sort of order, because this is how they have been socialised in all encounters with culture. Order will be of the chronological kind, or biased by the person in charge of organising the exhibition. In all cases it will be forced upon the individual. Only a few mavericks will stray away from the mainstream - sparking off outraged remarks - in order to look at that particular painting there. But basically everyone will follow the same pattern. This is because sequential thought patterns, for both accessing and transmitting knowledge, have been so deeply ingrained into the individual that there is no escape imaginable.

Now it is precisely through this lens, i.e., the discrepancy between sequential modes of access to knowledge, and random or direct modes, that the evolution of the document should be viewed. Throughout history and up to a relatively recent date, sequentiality has prevailed. In all tribal communities, the village storyteller maintained a single, linear string chaining the events he was telling. Oral speech does not allow for interaction, being essentially sequential, as any utterance is unique at one given moment in time. The Bible, the Scriptures, mostly born from oral traditions are also characterised by this straight, linear path which is to be found as well in any type of lecturing. Learners listening to a teacher have no alternative but to comply to his vision of things, his sense of history, his line of thought.

In other words, we tend to find this paradox absolutely normal, that in a didactic setting, the teaching approach should be exactly the reverse of that naturally assumed by the child in the playground. It seems as if for centuries we have placed the learner in the worst situation for learning. This is because of the inevitable sequentiality of any information presented.

The press is non-sequential

This is no longer entirely true. For example, examined as a document, the press today stands somewhere in-between the pure, hard-line sequentiality of the past and the elusive, randomised mode of access of the future. It actually works on a parallel basis, on some sort of complementary interaction between sequential and direct reading modes. This is the case for such news magazines as Newsweek, Time, etc. They target hurried readers whose attention must be captured, and then held captive to elicit purchase. Now these magazines, it should be noticed, are as much designed by layout specialists as written by expert journalists. Information is accessed visually as well as textually. The visual layout, respective size, content and positioning of the pictures in the left-right dynamics of the page are all elements informing the trained reader on whatever he is to find in the article. To the extent that he needn't read the article sequentially, but simply collect here and there any elements required for his information. In other words, when not reading for his pleasure, the efficient, modern reader often utilises a random, rather than linear mode of access to information.

71

Press advertising, when of the better kind, uses the same type of approach. The eyes of the reader are first and foremost those of a viewer guided towards elements capturing his sight and emotions in direct access, and gradually leading him to the copy, which rounds off the seductive operation by a more linear, intellectual argument.

Zapping is non-sequential

As is obvious, the trend is towards a retreat of the sequential mode. This is where a new phenomenon sets in, one that is nothing short of a revolution affecting how the media are both designed and consumed. The way parents watch TV is sequential: duly equipped with slippers and cup of coffee, a father will sit throughout his favourite soccer match or TV drama. The younger generation and the remote control have radically changed that. Zapping from one channel to the next actually boils down to taking information in random access, a process that is very close to that of the child in the playground. This is multiple tapping from a variety of sources which the child handles in a synecdochical way, i.e., by constantly reconstructing the whole from fragmented glimpses, so that he is capable of reading several programs at the same time. This is authentic competence, not something to be looked down upon.

Multimedias are sequential, Hypermedias are non-sequential

There is a general confusion between the terms of multimedia and hypermedia. In a multimedia environment, documents of the three kinds: textual, visual, audio, are loaded into a computer and easily accessible. But they are still organised in a sequential manner, like pages in a book, and in order to move from screen one to, say, screen four, the user has to go through the intermediate second and third screens in succession, even though they present no relevant information for him.

The emergence of hypermedia software applications in the wake of MPC technology allows for a presentation of information in successive layers which the user accesses directly, by targeting only the items he needs when he needs them, eliciting them on screen by pressing a button.

In a hypermedia document, certain areas - words, sentences, paragraphs or pictures - are designed as doors opening direct paths to other documents, other areas, other pictures. Those doors are activated by the user when clicking a button on the computer mouse. Granted, these paths have been paved by the person in charge of designing the application, who has inevitably used his own biased logic to integrate the variety of sources - texts, encyclopedic references, visuals - into a coherent information network. But it is for the reader himself to implement his own logic of access to information, according to his needs. There again, we are in the playground, not imprisoned in a book whose pages we are forced to thumb through one after the other.

The didactic implications are huge

This chronicle of a mutation to come, no matter how fascinating or scary, should not prevent us from reviewing the didactic issues at stake.

First of all it has considerable impact on learning. It is our belief that sequential transmission of information and knowledge, if used alone, is an elitist method of teaching. We have shown how opposed it is to the cognitive processes natural to the child. As a result, only those learners capable of gathering and using information presented in that manner, those capable of handling abstraction, i.e., the happy few trained from infancy by their family environment, will be in a position to handle it in such a form. The rest will only laboriously digest it, if at all. It is therefore obvious that those information technologies which are based on direct access will see new talents emerge amongst learners so far discarded by the very mode of access to knowledge.

Also, sequential learning results in intellectual standardisation, in that it is based on a one-way descent of information down to its target. On the contrary, as has been shown, random access to information preserves the user's personality.

Now for about one generation, teachers have been trying to re-define the rapport between the learner and knowledge. Admiration for the erudite has become obsolete, what matters is that intellectual energy must be devoted to the real tasks at hand. What matters is no longer to massively store facts, but to sort them, integrate them and reveal their relationships. The advent of CD-ROM dictionaries and encyclopaedias makes this extremely easy. As facts are now instantaneously accessible, they are no longer the first and foremost object of learning. Handling them is what matters. Therefore our role as teachers, more than ever, is to transmit skills, techniques and methodologies for accessing various data. Our role is to help students confront over-abundance, select appropriate paths through complex environments, and turn shreds of information into usable knowledge.

This does not preclude our traditional didactic concern, which consists in making students constantly move from high-guidance level activities, where they acquire methodology, to high-autonomy level activities, where they test and transfer their newly-acquired competence. As designers of these new tools, as well as facilitators for their use, we must be aware of all their properties and specificities, to make the best of them without betraying their logic - and reverting back to sequential modes, as is often seen.

School design will change

Another point, but certainly not the least, lies in the effect these instruments will have on the type of school space required to use them. As the teacher is no longer the only dispenser of knowledge, the traditional classroom will no longer be the only learning environment either. Conversely, the computer room, too large, noisy and collective, should not be the only place of contact with the computer. In between, language booths, or boxes or stalls, whatever they are called, housing two to three students operating a workstation on their own, will probably spread in institutions. They will enable students to explore, within their school time but out of their course time, both the access modes and the contents of the new documentary media.

73

Two ways to surf hypermedia applications

At that stage it is already possible to recommend two ways of navigating in a hypermedia application. One would derive from the traditional linear approach, based on strict Cartesian rigor, while the other would be random, based on the sheer pleasure principle. My first is objective-oriented research, whereby the students would be trained to first describe what they are looking for, what questions inspire their investigation, which research parameters they should define to either browse or interrogate the system - all questions, undeniably, of the very pedagogical sort.

My second is to simply enjoy the ride. Within reach of their keyboards, the students can open a genuine Ali Baba treasure cave, where all sorts of riches - texts, pictures, sound clips, all logically linked to each other - are just laying idle, waiting for activation of retrieval. The only obligation for the explorers would be to always be aware of where they are and how they got there. The quest may prove fortuitous, allowing them to access areas they would probably have left aside in an objective-oriented approach. This is serendipity at its best, i.e., the faculty to accidentally hit a bonanza; but the path there should always be marked carefully.

Both approaches have their advantages, and should of course be conducted in parallel.

The Net is a hypermedia

Such strategies remain valid when dealing with a far more impressive mass of objects, namely, those stored in the Information Highway, the Internet. Any recent encyclopaedia, Bookshelf, Encarta, etc., may be regarded as a microcosm of the Internet.

The quantities involved may change, as well as the cost of transporting the information, which is carried on the telephone network instead of moving within the same computer. But access poses exactly the same problems. In this perspective it is no doubt interesting to think about what to teach with the Internet as a hypermedia.

Net surfers are a hypermedia

The Net provides one extra, very exciting dimension. On the Net you can ask your way, not to a machine, not to a Windows help file, but to other human users on line. Suppose you teach to a class who is trying to find something specific, a name, the title of an Australian novel, a series of interviews on a particular subject. For various reasons - their needs are difficult to translate into keywords, the systems do not understand what they are looking for - your students have not been able to find out what they wanted. They can go over to one of these online forums where they can post their query in human words. Then they disconnect, and return to the same forum the next day, to find that people have left messages for them. Either definite answers or clues as to where to look for more. In other words, the people on the Net are an integral part of the information resources available out there.

In other terms, the pleasure of research is enhanced by the pleasure of communicating for real. The questions a student is asked in such an environment are authentic. This is no longer teacher questioning, whose answers are known and anticipated.

This is no pedagogical science-fiction - the scenario mentioned here has been realised with a setup comprising a computer and overhead projection panel, a modem, a subscription to Compuserve and a telephone line run through the classroom ceiling.

From Content to Methodology

One advantage of the hypermedia that we have not yet explored is that abstractions can be made concrete and visualised by easy access to pictures. Thus metaphors may be displayed on screen, mental processes such as unconscious grammatical operations can be translated into animations that are crystal-clear to the learner. Thus cultural data may be injected, in sound or visual form, within a perfectly user-friendly environment.

These reflections fed applications I designed as the outcome of participating in Workshop 7A in Paris, notably around the famous *"I have a dream"* speech by Martin Luther King, and around the Kennedy theme.

Such applications, I now realise, were content-oriented, i.e., they presented a document within a didactic environment whose major purpose was to enhance understanding and help learners access the meaning of a text which *per se* was the centre of the software proposed.

The very concept of hypermedia as described in these pages makes it an ideal tool for teaching strategies. So it seemed only logical to create methodology-oriented applications, whose documentary contents would only serve to exemplify exploratory techniques transferable to other documents. In other words, ideally, the hypermedia application would become an environment devoted to acquiring strategies whose various aspects the learner would absorb, whose validity he would assess in the *in vitro* shelter of the computer, before putting them to the *in vivo* test of reality when tackling any document of a comparable kind.

Reading Strategies in the Classroom

Over the years, having had to cater for VOLL students whose reading and writing skills are rather poor, I have developed a course on reading strategies whose principle is to create a systematic approach as to how to extract information from a *Newsweek*-type press page, which characteristically generates fear or mental blocks in the non-adept reader.

Confronted with a press article of that sort, the students should first anticipate its contents by a careful survey of what may be referred to as *peripheral information*, to be found in any pictures, charts, captions, titles and subtitles, places and dates, etc., surrounding the text itself.

Then, the method consists of systematically *highlighting* the sentences containing figures because they are easy to locate in any corpus, and because the journalist mentions them as evidence for his demonstration. Next should be underlined those containing quotes, for exactly the same reasons; then the first sentences of paragraphs, because they advertise their contents.

All of this highlighted data is turned into telegraphic-style notes on paper. Then comes the time to gather the data collected by the whole class. In my lecture room stands equipment comprising a PC and overhead projection panel. I run *Word* for *Windows*, and either I or any keyboard-fluent student becomes secretary, typing whatever information is dictated by the class.

In the final stage, before writing, *Word*'s outlining mode comes in to use, allowing for coherent re-ordering of a data whose journalese presentation usually goes against our Cartesian grain. Students intervene in English to justify positioning an element here rather than there. Once this is done we revert back to normal writing mode, and with the help of *Bookshelf* - the *Microsoft* CD-ROM encyclopaedia in direct access - we start the writing procedure proper, the *crafting* phase as it were. Along the powerful structural lines resulting from the previous task, we add the flesh of linkwords, verbs, adverbs, adjectives, relatives, and so forth.

Thus is implemented, collectively, an efficient reading strategy, followed by an organising reflection whose outcome is a writing task. This type of work does have palpable results, if only in notably alleviating the fear of reading complex articles.

Reading Strategies in a Hypermedia

This background work inevitably led me to design hypermedia applications that would enable students to consolidate such strategies. The idea was to continue working collectively as before, but also to tell those students who had the most difficulties in acquiring the strategies to go and do some solo training with the computer.

This definitely was of profit to the students. Simply because the hypermedia allows, through its visual and fast interaction features, to explain the different phases of the intellectual operations at play, far more efficiently than any teacher could do verbally.

How to build a methodology-oriented hypermedia

The work described above laid the basis for our group work in Karlsruhe. Our objectives were, for me to demonstrate the methodological application, for the group to test its theoretical validity, to develop and qualify the reflection, to produce another application along similar lines, and write recommendations on its effective use.

To the group I proposed a *Newsweek* article, with a mission to prepare its didactic environment with a hypermedia generator.

Building a didactic hypermedia improves didactic awareness

The team as a whole tested and recognised the validity of the strategy, but contributed an additional item to the approach. Readers, it was found, should also look for sentences *containing words already used in the peripheral information of the page, because they form networks carrying meaningful information related to the subject in question.*

Sub-groups were then formed, each with a specific task. One of them, after browsing my own image bank, which is related to *picture semiotics*, took care of analysing the visuals and captions on the page. They produced a very thorough, clear reflection which partly fed the work of yet another sub-group, who had tackled the audio aspect, i.e. introducing as a sound document what a native American reader might think aloud on entering the page. This could be called *native culture input.*

Our Danish colleague fed all textual information into the computer. I put this all into the Toolbook environment.The overall result was a nice piece of application which was sufficiently advanced to be shown at the plenary session. It is now on the CD-ROM which was released as the outcome of Workshop 9B.

As can be observed, the sub-groups' work was based on the principle that the computer was a tool, and pedagogy was the issue: *how can we use the resources of that thing to help students gain better methods of reading?*

At that stage an interesting phenomenon occurred. Only finalised, formalised teaching proposals could be turned into hypermedia. In other words, the sheer passage to computer form required precise work upstream. Objectives, as well as their concrete translations into actions taking place on screen, had to be clearly defined before the team came to me and said *this is what we want.*

This made us realise that very often in the language class, we tend to come along with ideas we work and sort out as they crop up, and we rely on class feedback to modify and adapt our input if it feels inadequate. The computer does not allow for such fuzziness.

I was so fascinated by the hypothesis that I tested it in the Académie of Rouen, where I was invited as teacher trainer for a one-day, one-man workshop on hypermedia in the language class. The group comprised 30 teacher-trainers of the very seasoned kind.

I played the *Toolbook* secretary again, and saw that some colleagues were extremely frustrated and aggressive when they found I was unable to make their ideas become "concrete" as it were. Only gradually did they realise that it was not the technology or my computer skills that were at fault - since their peers' proposals came out clear and successful on screen - but their ideas that were insufficiently worked out. They left the place with very thoughtful expressions on their faces.

Conclusion

The obvious conclusion is that in both initial and on-job training, using a hypermedia generator as a training facilitator should be very profitable. One or two teacher trainers, fluent in the software and well-versed in didactics, could have a group of trainees work not on IT *per se*, but on pedagogical strategies transferable onto the computer. This would show that what matters is not so much the technical object as the clarity of the teaching approaches using it. It would also show the sceptics, from the start, that the tool is efficient - when there's a brain behind it, as has always been the case.

5. EXPLOITATION OF MATERIALS IN A HYPERTEXT ENVIRONMENT - GASTRONOMIC FRENCH

Aagot ELSLANDE - Norway

The work in the Research and Development group

The hypertext group which was established at Workshop 9B in Grimstad had the advantage of working together to develop their applications. Most the members of the group were living in the Oslo area, but the most important factor was that the Norwegian Government made it possible for the members of the group to get together for several working sessions. This opportunity to solve problems together was very useful and made it possible to find ways around many obstacles. The fact that we could take advantage of the experience of all the members of the group created considerable enthusiasm for the project. All the members contributed, we could profit from the insight and the creativity of the other members and especially from the audio expertise of one of the members. These gatherings were made possible by funding from the Norwegian government and the initiative of the Norwegian group leader.

All the members of the group created applications for the student groups with whom they were working, and since I teach beginner's level French to Hotel and Catering students, my obvious choice was to create an application for them.

French for Hotel and Catering and the typical student

The French language is of great importance in the catering business in Norway. Modern Norwegian catering is to a large extent based upon the French gastronomic tradition and this manifests itself in different ways, not least through the many French loanwords into the Norwegian professional language.

The typical vocational student often finds foreign languages difficult. It is not his or her personal study choice in the first place, and this manifests itself in a lack of motivation. However, the student in the hotel and catering business will get acquainted with quite a lot of the French expressions when working in the kitchen and also in most of the subject matter lessons. Thus the learning of French is supported by a previously acquired insight attached to the secrets of the trade.

This is an important factor which can be exploited in a language learning situation among students with poor knowledge of language in general and with low self esteem in relation to their capacity for language acquisition.

Description of the hypertext

At the beginning of the application the reader is invited to enter a restaurant and study the menu. In the last section of the hypertext the reader is invited to write down what he has chosen from the menu and print it out.

The different sections of this hypertext are separate but linked together. The reader can only navigate within the section chosen. The hypertext is designed in this way to match the standard of the computer used in the classroom.

There are six different sections: *Hors-d'oeuvre, Potage, Poisson, Viandes et gibier, Dessert, Votre Commande.*

The design of the different screens is void of superfluous information. This is done so that the reader can focus upon the process of reading rather than the interactivity of the computer itself. All the screens of one section have the same design, the choice of colour gives information in itself, the backgrounds have all the same colour, so have the textfields and the buttons. When the textfield exceeds the size of the screen, a scrollbar is used. Hotwords are put into the text for explanations or for further information about a topic.

The window of the application is thus designed with little extraneous information and few effects. This is done to focus upon the language and to take the attention away from the effect of the design.

The typical reader is a beginner of French and often an illustration is a better way to indicate the meaning of a word than a explanatory text containing difficult words and concepts. In gastronomic language this is particularly true - a dish is easily explained by an illustration.

The sound in this application is activated by radiobuttons recognisable by a label of "Pronunciation".

The texts in the application are composed with a large number of transparent words, that is, words that are similar in French and in Norwegian or recognisable as similar for the student in the catering business. Due to the frequency of transparent words the reader can understand an otherwise rather advanced text.

The reader navigates through the texts by pressing a button. In this way the reader decides the speed needed to read the text.

The button marked *Potages* gives access to the following text:

> Potage de pois cassés
> Potage Parmentier
> Potage Solférino
> Soupe à la tomate

Consommé de volaille
Consommé chasseur
Crème d'asperges

This list of dishes is composed to give the reader different examples of linguistic structures. The list contains the different types of *potages* like *crème, soupe, consommé* and the reader will find hotwords to explain the difference between these soups when this is relevant. As the gastronomic expressions also reveal the origin of the dishes or other cultural aspects of a country's history, some of the hotwords also indicate this. The text is meant to give the student some knowledge of the "cuisine" and thereby an insight into the culture of another country.

The linguistic structure is also different in most of these expressions. We notice that *crème* is followed by the preposition *de*, *soupe* is followed by the preposition *à* and some soups contain no preposition, like the expression *Potage Parmentier*. The text does not really explain the difference between these constructions, but the reader will get acquainted with the existence of the variety of expressions.

Mr Parmentier, as it is explained in the hotword was an important historical person in the 18th century in Paris. The student who is training to become cook or waiter may, by reading this, be able to see the historical links of the trade and the importance of the trade from a new angle. This is the idea behind these texts: by choosing this path through the application the student will become aware of the origins and the importance of the traditions of the trade.

A similar example is the *Potage Solférino*. Of course there are several anecdotes indicating the origin of this expression, but they all focus on the Napoleonic wars and they are included in this text for the same reason as mentioned above. By combining language learning with knowledge of the trade and general history I believe that the students can be helped to develop a certain pride in the tradition of the gastronomic profession.

The following words in the text are also used in a purely Norwegian context and are thus already known to the student: *potage, soupe, Parmentier, Solférino, tomate, consommé, crème, chasseur*. With this in mind the text should not be too difficult for the average student and they should be able to read the text with the aid of the hotwords and by guessing or working with the text. The hotwords for this text give an explanation, but they are also composed of a text with a similar level of difficulty. The student will know some of the words but not all, and the text is supported by illustrations to enhance the comprehension process.

An author of a text must, of course, decide upon the quantity of hotwords in the text of a specific screen. The conscientious reader might easily press all the hotwords and read all the texts, which would constantly interrupt the reading of the page itself. Thus to prevent the reader from jumping constantly from one page to another the number of hotwords on each page was limited.

81

Some examples of hotwords and hotword texts:

Chasseur is the hotword.

The text in the hotword window:

Chasseur se dit d'apprêts sautés, accompagnés d'une sauce aux champignons à l'échalote au vin blanc et à la tomate. La même sauce peut aussi être servie avec des oeufs sur le plat ou fourrer une omelette.

The reader will recognise most of the key words in this text and thus be able to read it.

Another principle for composing the text in a hotword window is illustrated by the case of the textword attached to the hotword *crème aspèrge*. The students know, or are believed to know, how a *crème* is prepared. If they utilise this knowledge, the text may be understood. However, if they do not know how to make a *crème*, the text would need some work to be understood.

Crème d'asperges
Une crème est un potage au fond blanc, lié à la farine. L'élément de base est souvent fourni par un légume.

To explain to the student why there are different words to express *soupe* is a difficult task, the explanation is complex and it is connected to French history. In the hotword we have chosen an aspect from social history. The illustration to this hotword underlines this by showing a young woman from the working class with her bowl of soup. Illustrations of this kind are chosen to make the student curious about the cultural background,

The hotword to explain *soupe*:

---

*A l'origine **la soupe** était une tranche de pain sur laquelle on versait du bouillon, du vin ou une sauce. Aujourd'hui la soupe est un potage ni passé, ni lié, mais épaissi par du pain, des pâtes, du riz, garni de viande ou de poisson et de légumes divers.*

Even though the focus is on language learning and reading in a professional context, a hypertext of this kind allows one to add information that might be considered extraneous or even disturbing in an ordinary textbook. The interactive dimension allows the reader to choose a path of interest, and this should be stressed when the students are introduced to the hypertext. Thus, although not all the students will read all the information, hotwords will hopefully be chosen according to interest or curiosity.

Another very important benefit of the hypertext application is the opportunity to hear the text read by a native speaker. The hypertext is an integrated application of text, illustration and sound. The student can press a small button and listen to the chosen expression in French. When designing the sound, we chose to divide it into minor soundfiles because the correct pronunciation of gastronomic expressions is the first need of these students. As the sound takes up a lot of space, an application matching the kind of PC the students have access to was chosen.

Each section in the hypertext functions in the manner described above. The application consists of several sections representing parts of a menu and when reading one particular part, *poisson* for instance, the reader can look up the hotwords here. There might also be hotwords attached to the text of the hotword itself, but the reader is always taken back to the section he is studying when closing the hotword. This way the student can continue the original text once the hotword is read, which ensures that the student actually studies the text and not only surfs from page to page without reading.

Even at this early stage, the students' level of French varies considerably. This is why texts have been included which would otherwise have been too difficult for the mainstream student. These texts are placed in hotwords since hotword texts are optional. One example of these advanced texts is the text giving information about Mr. Parmentier. This text is quite elaborate and the average student would not be advised to read it.

ANTOINE AUGUSTIN PARMENTIER,
(1737 - 1813), pharmacien et agronome français.

Prisonnier de guerre à Westphalen pendant la guerre de Sept Ans, Parmentier a découvert la valeur de la pomme de terre et depuis il favorisa la culture de ce légume en France. Après la grande famine en 1786 le roi a mis une fleur de pomme de terre dans sa boutonnière et Parmentier a fait planter des pommes de terre à plusieurs endroits en France, pour faciliter la diffusion de la pomme de terre aux populations encore méfiantes. Les cultures parisiennes sont gardées militairement de jour, mais non de nuit, et c'est ainsi que les gens qui viennent s'en approvisionner clandestinement sont devenus des propagandistes les plus efficaces de ce nouveau légume.

*L'appellation **"Parmentier"** s'applique en particulier aux plats préparés avec la pomme de terre. Un potage Parmentier est une crème de pommes de terre.*

When this text is visible in the hotword, only the advanced student will find the text interesting, but average and less advanced students will be able to study the illustrations in the hotword. In this way both groups can find something of interest in the same window.

The last section of this hypertext-application is simply a page where the student is asked to write down what he has chosen from the menu and place an order to an imagined waiter. In this section the student must not only read the text or listen to the native speaker reading the text, but he must think of the correct spelling as well. Some will even compose a nice and correct menu.

There is no spellchecker in this section, only a button to print out the order. It would be easy to develop the application further by linking a spellchecker to this window.

A further development of the application would be to add a dictionary for the student to use when producing his own texts.

In some of the hotwords we have focused on understanding simply by showing an illustration. An example is in the fish-section. Types of fish usually create some misunderstanding among the students, and a complicating factor is the fact that species of fish vary considerably from region to region. This has lead us to the solution chosen here, the hotword "anguille" only contains a photo of the type of fish.

The hypertext is constructed for the student to read through in a linear way, ie. the student would have to read all the sections of the menu to be able to place an order for the dinner, but within each section the student can choose what hotwords to look into and which ones to avoid. It was important for us to use a design that ensures that the student actually reads through the text.

In this application, I have not made full use of the possibilities for making completely non-linear text, allowing for more choice. I believe that the less advanced students will enjoy reading more where a combination of choice and guidance is possible.

Implementation in the classroom

The students worked in pairs. As the texts contained quite a number of new words, a lot of guessing and interpretation went on. Working in pairs helped to minimise the differences between the groups.

The hypertext application gave each student the opportunity to read more than would be possible in a traditional classroom. Within the framework of the same text the students studied at different levels. The application allowed the reader autonomy - the student decided how to read the application and which texts to study further. The interactive aspect, the idea that the reader must choose and actively push a button to work through the text, was a motivating factor for most of the students. Thus the non-linear hypertext was in itself an aspect increasing the motivation of the reader. The reader took full control over the texts by choosing his way through them, avoiding what he didn't want to read. In the hypertext solution it is never a question of how many pages the students have managed to read, but more what the students have chosen to read. Thus the problem with slow readers did not manifest itself as a relevant one. The hypertext gave the student a notion of equality in relation to the text they chose to work with. What increased the students' motivation more than anything else, was probably the fact that they considered themselves autonomous and in control of their own learning process.

References

Aasgaaarden/Otnes (1995) "De gamle guder på gjesting", *Norsklæreren* nr 5.
Ramberg K. /EDB-tjenesten HF UIT (1992) Å tenke med tastaturet. En teori om hypertekst illustrert med eksempler fra en hypertekst om norrøn mytologi.
Schwebs, T. (1994) "Hypertekstualitet", *Norsklæreren* nr 2.
Schwebs, T. (1994) "Litteraturundervisning som rullett", *Norsklæreren* nr 5.
Vikingbyen, Norsk læremiddelsenter, DOS-prosjekt.

Internet:

http://www.skolevien.telenor.no/
http://odin.nls.no/viking/nvnethome.htm
http://control.chalmers.se/vikings/viking.htlm
http://cutt.city.unisa.edu.au/pub/windows/toolbook/
ftp.ibn.fr/pub6/pc/win3/toolbook/

6. LEMMATIZED CONCORDANCES OF COMPLEX UTTERANCES: APPLICATION TO LANGUAGE LEARNING

Mylène GARRIGUES - France

From manual methods to computer methods

Preparation of concordances consists in finding every occurrence of a word within a given corpus, and then grouping them according to context.

Concordances are not new: the first were on the Bible, and were aimed at enabling comparison between different versions in order to reach a standardised editorial version. (see concordances by Birckman, 1567, or Passelecq and Poswick, 1974, compiled several centuries apart).

Such concordances were of course prepared by hand, and until recently there was no other possible method of processing texts in general. This exercise is crucial for many activities: searching for examples in lexicography, studying the contexts of a word or a semantic field in the work of a particular author or in a particular literary work (the theme of *'regard'* in Baudelaire, for example). However, the time invested in the strictly manual part of the task is disproportionate to that spent analysing the lists and groupings obtained.

Computers now make the manual method almost obsolete, for two reasons:

- firstly, more and more corpora of texts (*AFP* dispatches, *Le Monde* newspaper, literary works, etc.) are available on electronic media (diskettes, hard disks and especially CD-ROM) and provide the general public with extensive databases;

- secondly, software tools make it possible to search for words or groups of words in these texts with just one command, and at speeds which were unthinkable just a few years ago (a few seconds by machine as opposed to months or even years manually!).

Figure 1 gives examples of concordances for the word *enseignement(s)* which were extracted automatically in a few seconds from a one-day AFP corpus (116,000 words of text).

Applications have consequently increased and continue to do so. Among such applications, it is now possible to envisage the use of concordances in language teaching (Rézeau, 1988; Johns and King, 1991). Interest in this area of research is regularly demonstrated, as shown by the number of articles and conferences on the subject[1] and by the work of one of the Council of Europe Workshop 7B groups.

Il préconise également l'	enseignement	de la langue anglaise comme deuxième la
réconise des échanges d'ordre culturel (	enseignement	du français par exemple à Dheishé) et h
rencontres, d'échanges d'expériences, d'	enseignement	et de recherche sur la médecine à dista
vention des accidents du travail dans l'	enseignement	technique a été officiellement mis en p
chaque jour en France. Et le monde de l'	enseignement	technique, fréquenté par près de 1,2 mi
vin et le secrétaire d'Etat chargé de l'	enseignement	technique Robert Chapuis.
s / Mieux prévenir les accidents dans l'	enseignement	technique
sur la prévention des accidents dans l'	enseignement	technique sera présenté au Conseil des
, M. Lajoinie a jugé qu'il y avait des "	enseignements	à tirer de l'activité des communistes d

Figure 1 - concordances for the word *enseignement(s)*: AFP

Which computer tools for which concordances?

The reference function

The basic 'grep' or 'search' function present in many operating systems or professional software packages (word processing, for instance) is the basis of the 'concordance' function, as it allows a word to be found in a text as many times as it occurs. As the word to be found is considered here merely as a character sequence, the system does not use **a dictionary** nor **any grammatical analysis**. Thus:

- a search for the word *mange* surrounded by a space on either side amounts to finding the character sequence *m,a,n,g,e*. This search cannot locate any form other than *mange*;

- a search for the same character sequence but not surrounded by spaces would locate the infinitive *manger* and all verb forms containing the sequence *m,a,n,g,e*. It would also locate derivatives such as *mangeoire* and compound words such as *mange-tout*. But this development also brings disadvantages: the same search would supply **noises**, since it would include words like *dé(mange)aisons*, and **silences**, as it would ignore forms such as *mangiez* or *mangés*.

Educational software

'Concordancers', or software for educational applications of this function, and the current operating tools that come with textual databases, offer a more effective version of the 'grep' function. Thanks to the improvements offered, they can give rise to a number of very useful applications in language classes. However, they do have limits which an uninformed public cannot immediately discern. Those limits are primarily related to the **absence of dictionaries** (an absence which is sometimes presented as an advantage!). To give an idea of these limits, we will discuss three points:

---

[1] For example, the TALC conference: TALC 96 "Teaching and Language Corpora". Lancaster University, UK, 9-12 August 1996.

lemmatisation

If we wanted to use this software to find all the occurrences of the verb *être* in a text, we would have to search for each inflected form one by one: *suis, sommes, serions, furent, été*, etc. and then group them manually under the lemmatised form (or generic form) *être*. As the automatic word recognition process does not use a coded dictionary, the software cannot carry out automatic lemmatisation.

the variables

The search process can be improved through the use of variables (truncations or jokers). These may be inserted to the left or right of part of a word or within a word, and operate on a specified or unspecified number of letters. We could thus ask it to search, for example, for:

-   all words beginning with *cerv* and followed by a specified or unspecified number of letters (*cerv???* or *cerv**) or

-   all words finishing with *eau* and preceded by a specified or unspecified number of letters (*????eau* or **eau*) or

-   all words with a common skeleton and a specified or unspecified number of variable letters (*cha?elle* or *cha*elle*).

Although they improve the search process, these variables do not eliminate noises or silences. On the contrary:

In the first case, from *cerv???* we would obtain cerv(eau) but not *cerveaux*, whereas for *cerv** we would obtain *cerveau, cerveaux*, but also *cervelle, cervelas, cervical* etc. Generally, the effectiveness of the process varies according to the length of the syllables given: the shorter the syllables, the less effective the process.

grammatical categories

If, as many language teachers would do, we wanted to find the occurrences not of a word but of a grammatical category such as *adjective, preposition, verb* etc., this could only be done by searching concordances of each adjective, preposition or verb one by one, and we would need to have been able to draw up a list of them beforehand! It would be even less feasible to search for syntactic structures, as the system presented below allows us to do.

Tools for automatic processing of natural languages

Automatic processing of natural languages necessitates the development of highly formalised linguistic tools. Although they are not specifically designed for language teaching, such tools can be very useful. In this way we used the *Intex* system (Silberztein, 1990) to prepare concordances. Without going into details, it operates both a huge set of electronic dictionaries of simple words (80,000), compound words (150,000), etc. in which each entry is accompanied by a morphosyntactic code (Courtois and Silberztein, 1991), and electronic grammars which are easily implemented with the help of a program editor incorporated into the system.[1]

The system is simple to use: from the start the user has access to two menus, one for the automatic preparation of corpus sub-dictionaries and the other for automatic searching for words or word sequences in texts. Within each menu, the user clicks on a button to execute a search by the machine on any text previously loaded.

To illustrate the first application, we entered the script of a few minutes of a TV film (*L'amour est un jeu d'enfant, 1994*) into the computer. (see fig. 2)

Non Monsieur Ancelot ! c'était 9 h. 1/2 ! C'était bien précisé sur la note d'information qui vous a été adressée, ainsi qu'à toutes les familles d'ailleurs !
Bon, ben moi je croyais que c'était 10 h. 1/2, voilà, hein. Eh, Benjamin, Benjamin, Benjamin, oh !
Ah ! tu es là Papa !
he he he ! ça va mon bonhomme ?
Qu'est-ce que peut bien faire Madame Fournet, une femme si sérieuse, si organisée !
Ah je ne comprends pas.
Ma maman est toujours pas là ?
C'est pas grave ! On va te ramener chez toi. Hein ? tu n'as qu'à venir avec nous. On va la ramener, hein, Papa ? elle habite pas très loin de chez nous.
Sinon je serais obligée d'appeler le commissariat. C'est toujours très traumatisant pour un enfant.
Je veux pas aller au commissariat.
Ben écoute, je ne sais pas moi euh, tu sais pas où elle est ta maman ?
Elle doit dormir. Le samedi matin c'est toujours moi qui la réveille, alors, mais je veux pas aller au commissariat.
S'il te plaît !
Dis donc, il est sympa, ton père.
Tu crois qu'il plaira à ta mère ?
Ben, c'est pas tout à fait le même genre si tu vois ce que je veux dire.
Ouais, nous non plus, on n'était vraiment pas du même genre, en arrivant au stage.
Maintenant pour moi tu es déjà ma petite soeur.
C'est là.
A quel étage ?
Au dernier, là haut;
Avec la terrasse ?
Oui, attendez-moi, je vais voir.
Putain, dis donc ils s'emmerdent pas, hein. Qu'est-ce qu'ils font ses parents ?
Je sais pas, des affaires je crois

Figure 2 - script of film extract

---

[1]   All of these tools are developed at LADL (Laboratoire d'Automatique Documentaire et Linguistique) - Paris 7, directed by Professor Maurice Gross.

We then asked for the dictionary of simple words in this text with the grammatical label corresponding to each entry (fig. 3), and then for the dictionary of compound words in the text (fig. 4). Other requests are also possible and require just as little time (a few seconds): word frequency, dictionary of adjectives, verbs or adverbs for example.

a	N:ms:mp
à	PREP
a	XI
absolument	ADV
accident	N:ms
accord	N:ms
acheter	V:F2s,V:W
actuellement	ADV
adressé	A:fs
adresse	N:fs
adresser	V:Kfs,V:P1s:P3s:S1s:S3s:Y2s
affaire	N:fp,N:fs
affairer	V:P1s:P3s:S1s:S3s:Y2s,V:P2s:S2s
affaires	N:fp
agréable	A:ms:fs,N:ms
ah	INTJ
aider	V:W
ailler	V:P1s:P3s:S1s:S3s:Y2s
ailleurs	ADV
aime	N:mp,N:ms
aimer	V:C1s:C2s,V:P3p:S3p,V:P1s:P3s:S1s:S3s:Y2s,V:P2s:S2s
ainsi	ADV
ajouter	V:G
allégé	A:mp,A:ms
alléger	V:Kmp,V:Kms
aller	V:F3s,V:P2p:Y2p,V:P3s,V:P3s:Y2s,V:P2s,V:P1s,V:S1s:
alors	ADV
amène	A:ms:fs
amener	V:P1s:P3s:S1s:S3s:Y2s
amour	N:ms
amusé	A:mp
amuser	V:Kmp
an	N:ms
année	N:fs
annonce	N:fs
annoncer	V:P1s:P3s:S1s:S3s:Y2s

Figure 3 - dictionary of simple words

boucherie chevaline	boucherie chevaline	N;NA:fs -+;une
conte de fée	conte de fée	N;NDN:ms -+;un
coup d'oeil	coup d'oeil	N;NDN:ms -+;un
coup de foudre	coup de foudre	N;NDN:ms -+;un
flocons d'avoine	flocons d'avoine	N;NDN:mp --;des
jeu d'enfant	jeu d'enfant	N;NDN:ms -+;un
jus d'orange	jus d'orange	N;NDN:ms --;de&le
numéro de téléphone	numéro de téléphone	N;NDN:ms -+;un
petit déjeuner	petit déjeuner.	N;AN:ms --;le
petit frère	petit frère	N;AN:ms -+;un
petite copine	petite copine	N;AN:fs -+;une
petite fille	petite fille	N;AN:fs -+;une
petite soeur	petite soeur	N;AN:fs -+;une
stage de voile	stage de voile	N;NDN:ms -+;un
Trésor public	Trésor Public	N;NA:ms --;le
Trésor public	Trésor public	N;NA:ms --;le
trésor public	trésor public	N;NA:ms --;le

Figure 4 - dictionary of compound words

One possible use of these functions is the precise evaluation of vocabulary or syntactic structures to which learners have been exposed during a lesson or set of lessons. The size of the corpus does not pose any problem once the corpus is on magnetic or optic media.

Another type of concordance

The second application makes it possible to create concordances ranging from the simplest case (a word) to the most complex (a grammar). We will illustrate this hierarchy with searches we carried out on a variety of texts:

i.   Search for a word and its inflected forms

We asked for concordances of the verb *poser* in a corpus of texts by entering only this canonical form. The result, 42 occurrences, was obtained in a few seconds and gives, as may be observed in the sample presented in figure 5, the conjugated forms found in the text.

The right- and/or left-hand contexts may be defined within the limits of an A4 page.

plus saisissante, la plus sensible, mais également la moins	posée	, est celle du type de société, d'environnement, de mode de
effets eux aussi très différents. La question la plus aiguë	posée	par l'introduction de microorganismes recombinés dans la na
cile question : "les machines peuvent-elles penser ?" a été	posée	par un scientifique, A. Turing dans un texte désormais célè
onde. Différences confirmées Si nous revenons à la question	posée	plus haut, qui est de savoir si les mégapoles du Sud sont
s bases pour la constitution d'un nouveau paradigme ont été	posées	, encore une fois, par l'apparition d'une nouvelle épistémé
aire pouvait-elle aider à répondre aux questions nombreuses	posées	par le cerveau et qui ont suscité tant de polémiques : rela
ience du risque biotechnologique (Annexe 11) Les questions	posées	par le développement des technologies du vivant sont, en fa
e cette "boite à outil" sont multiples et les questions que	posent	ces applications sont loin d'être résolues. Cette instrumen
ance approfondie des futures caractéristiques d'un individu	posent	dès lors des problèmes importants concernant le stockage e
ts). Les applications de ces recherches au secteur agricole	posent	des problèmes généraux de gestion des écosystèmes qui, dans
ostures des individus, mais, simultanément, les savants qui	posent	les problèmes et inventent les réponses, baignent dans notr
passe dans la réalité, afin de traiter les problèmes qui se	posent	ou peuvent se poser à fond, à froid, à temps. Une démarche
etc...). Ces techniques de recombinaison génétique végétale	posent	plusieurs problèmes, notamment celui de la fixation des car
, afin de traiter les problèmes qui se posent ou peuvent se	poser	à fond, à froid, à temps. Une démarche associative qui ass
mpli qui est facteur de démotivation. Planifier c'est donc	poser	à l'avance les problèmes techniques, économiques et sociaux
en mer; Ces derniers pouvaient réagir par radio-téléphone ,	poser	des questions, donner des nouvelles, toutes choses réutilis
L'évaluation des risques. La première question qui peut se	poser	est celle du caractère pathogène des microorganismes utilis
dans le recours à la notion de transcendant, qui permet de	poser	la source du pouvoir en dehors de la société des hommes. Ce
ière entièrement nouvelle de considérer les problèmes ou de	poser	les questions, reste hors de toute prévision. Aucune action
ge de ces terrains trop plats ; et des questions peuvent se	poser	quant aux exclusives ethniques (parfois) et quand aux contr
à de nouveaux déluges, en attente de nouvelles "terres" où	poser	: il faudra bien, après avoir identifié les touches, comme
u-delà de la localisation, la question du fonctionnement se	posera	à l'échelle de la planète, les problèmes rencontrés par les
pérer que vers 2010 ou 2020, cet objectif étant atteint, se	poseront	par l'appréciation des risques du SIDA par la recherche d
atal. 13 Mai 1985. Avis concernant les problèmes éthiques	posés	par la lutte contre la diffusion de l'infection par le vi
locaux. 16 Décembre 1988. Avis sur les problèmes éthiques	posés	par le développement des méthodes d'utilisation de cellul
et scientifiques. 23 Février 1987. Avis sur les problèmes	posés	par le diagnostic prénatal et périnatal. 13 Mai 1985. A
s et de prévention. 13 Mai 1985. Avis sur les problèmes	posés	par les essais de nouveaux traitements chez l'homme. Réfl
s et scientifiques. 9 octobre 1984. Problèmes d'éthique	posés	

Figure 5 - concordance of the verb *poser*

ii. Search for a grammatical category

As the system dictionaries contain morphosyntactic information, it is possible to ask for concordances of different grammatical categories: verb, noun, adjective, conjunction etc. We asked first for concordances of simple adverbs (fig. 6) and then compound adverbs (fig. 7) in a *Le Monde* newspaper corpus.

u'il brûle contient du soufre! De 0,2 %	actuellement	, la teneur en soufre sera obligatoireme
l reste que le gros problème du gazole,	actuellement	, réside dans les caractéristiques très
igeant en indice d'octane. Il deviendra	ainsi	sensible à l'auto-allumage et pourra êt
amment, sur le dos des consommateurs.	Alors	, depuis trois ans, Renault et PSA ont d
'autres s'en remettent au sans-plomb 98	alors	que du sans-plomb 95 leur suffirait.
bles quantités délivrées en accroissent	anormalement	le prix. Logiquement, il devrait y avoi
mmateur et l'environnement. Deux causes	apparemment	assez péremptoires pour faire très rapi
faisant à nos exigences. Or, trois ans	après	, le ministère des Finances n'a toujours
'environnement. Deux causes apparemment	assez	péremptoires pour faire très rapidement
ement à un objectif technologique, mais	aussi	à de sévères normes anti-pollutio
es modélisations plus simples mais tout	aussi	irréfutables. Pour ce test particulier,
aurait les mêmes effets et éloignerait	aussi	le spectre des émissions cancérigènes.
nt endommagées parce que l'usager a cru	bien	faire en faisant le plein au sans-plomb
e sans plomb iront s'accroissant, c'est	bien	l'Eurosuper 95 qu'il faudra inéluctable
1 ! Il n'empêche, les pétroliers sont	bien	malvenus de récupérer à leur profit la
comme acceptables sur ce point précis,	bien	que les mesures ont relevé de substanci
ntérêts commerciaux, il est inutilement	cher	et sophistiqué, au point d'être injusti
ent l'essence jusqu'à 60 centimes moins	cher	le litre ! "Même si elles nous soumettai
blement détergente parvienne à nettoyer	complètement	un moteur déjà encrassé: elle peut, par
n'est pas non plus acquis qu'une esence	convenablement	détergente parvienne à nettoyer complèt
combustion. Et ils n'ont pas forcément	davantage	de vertus curatives universelles: tel m
ienne à nettoyer complètement un moteur	déjà	encrassé: elle peut, par exemple, y par

Figure 6 - concordance of simple adverbs (continued on next page)

93

	demain	, le panorama risque d'être encore plus
95 leur suffirait. D'autant plus que,	donc	dû à des approvisionnements de qualité
itaine, mais aussi dans l'Est. Il était	donc	édicté leur propre cahier des charges.
es anti-pollution. Renault et PSA ont	encore	que pour les moteurs à essence, ces ver
erformances et d'agrément. Mais, plus	encore	trop peu sévères. Ce constat a fait gra
, que les constructeurs jugent pourtant	Enfin	, ils ont obtenu gain de cause sur les t
ondent sur des paramètres volumiques.	étroitement	liées à la qualité du gazole. Renault e
les moteurs à essence, ces vertus sont	éventuellement	du rôle lubrifiant du plomb pour la ten
nt besoin d'un indice d'octane de 97 et	éventuellement	retrouver sa propreté au niveau des sou
ncrassé par une mauvaise essence pourra	éventuellement	super 98, sans plomb seulement, quel
per plombé seulement, super plombé ou	facilement	dans la chambre de combustion, ce qui d
ange gazeux air-carburant pénètre moins		

Figure 6 (continued) - concordance of simple adverbs

cement de l'enseignement privé ? L'avenir le dira	à brève échéance	. En attendant, il est permis de s'amuser du parad
s ", qui a été interrompue le 21 novembre dernier	à cause de	la fermeture, pour travaux, du Grand Palais. Cett
re est diminuée de 8 % par rapport aux prévisions	à cause de	la sécheresse (elle ne devrait plus être que de 1
cettes du tourisme avaient chuté de 40 % environ,	à cause des	attentats. Eh bien, ici, sans attentat, on est dé
n Ouganda, où " beaucoup d'enfants sont orphelins	à cause du	sida ". Face aux mille souffrances, physiques
cidité est bien courte et démoralisante, parce qu'	à ce compte-là	, étant tous mortels, on pourrait vivre n'importe
ivité sur l'emploi. Les chiffres les plus récents	à ce sujet	indiquent pourtant de nombreuses créations d'empl
isions des Douze, la dernière instruction en date	à ce sujet	prise par la Communauté remontant à septembre der
er l'immigration clandestine mais de l'organiser.	A cet effet	, un accord a été signé à Jakarta, le 15 décembre,
que l'Histoire attend le personnel politique et,	à cet égard	, le député de la Dordogne ne s'est pas particuliè
la stratégie. On ne peut plus caractéristique est	à cet égard	leur attitude à l'égard du drame yougoslave. Comm
espagnole des AGF, et sur la montée en puissance,	à cette occasion	, des AGF dans la nouvelle structure. En moin
s de titres dont 231 milliards de francs de BTAN.	A cette occasion	, tous nos voeux vont à Sylvain de Forges, patron
fini par aboutir et l'Union européenne a retrouvé	à cette occasion	une cohésion dont, à la lumière du brasier yougos
dont s'y est pris Henri Konan Bédié pour assumer	à chaud	la succession de Félix Houphouët-Boigny. Et l'on

Figure 7 - concordance of compound adverbs

iii. Search for a syntactic structure

The choice 'rational utterance' allows searching for any syntactic structure. For example, we asked the computer to search a text for verbs followed by a prepositional infinitive introduced by *à* or *de*, using the expression:
<V>(*à*+*de*)<V:W>

We can see that the structure requested can combine specific words (*à*) and grammatical categories which may or may not be accompanied by morphological specifications (V for verb or V:W for verb in the infinitive). (see fig. 8, extract from the result, 22 occurrences)

iv. Search for a local grammar

A graph editor makes it possible to express local grammars in the form of automata (or graphs). This formalisation system (Gross, 1989) permits recognition of all occurrences of a given grammar in any text. This method of formalisation may be applied to any linguistic, lexical or syntactic phenomenon with, depending on the purpose of the application, very varied degrees of complexity (Maurel, 1989; Garrigues, 1993).

, à disparaître. Le libéralisme sauvage	aspire à extraire	l'individu de son milieu
amais être utilisé tant qu'on n'est pas	assuré de maîtriser	tous ses effets. De telle:
eloppé par le livre de Michel Serres, s'	attache à développer	, pour le rapport homme
se et emperière de l'univers" ? Pascal,	attaché à souligner	la finitude humaine, se
re de sa "volonté de puissance", qui la	conduit à mettre	les connaissances qu'el
ions La science est cette démarche qui	consiste à élucider	les lois du monde réel a
ssement des sciences et des arts a-t-il	contribué à épurer	les moeurs ?" (1750) Et
lle, celle qu'il faut tant bien que mal	essayer de comprendre	pour mieux l'habiter. O
ire dans l'utilisation de techniques (c'	est-à-dire	de savoir-faire détermir
ique, mais ausqsi et surtout sagesse, c'	est-à-dire	disposition à agir dans l
patible avec le respect de la nature, c'	est-à-dire	en fin de compte lucide
aussi de ses limites ; une technique (c'	est-à-dire	un savoir transformé en
r dans le coût réel d'un produit ?). Il	est à parier	qu'une prise en compte
ogrès ? Pour dénouer l'ambiguité, force	est de préciser	le sens de la question, v
propre au rationnalisme philosophique,	invite à poser	clairement la question d
e qu'elle évolue. A tout le moins, cela	invite à réfléchir	, à tout moment, sur la p
ence, et leur plasticité éducative leur	permet de conquérir	ce dont ils ne disposent
enrichie de l'analyse systématique, qui	permet de dresser	un bilan méthodique de
n harmonie avec elle, d'en tirer ce qui	permet de vivre	(est-ce "bien vivre que i

Figure 8 - concordance of the requested syntactical structure

The order of third-person pronouns is a compulsory step in learning French morphosyntax. It would thus be legitimate to look for examples of corresponding syntactic configurations in texts in order to base exercises on them. To do this, a program has to be constructed to enable the computer to recognise and group together all occurrences of that structure. We did this as an example:

The program in figure 9 represents a grammar of the order of third-person personal pronouns preceded by some kind of pronoun and followed by a verb. The graph is read from left to right, and any route that goes from the beginning of the program to the end corresponds to an authorised combination. Thus, the route "*PRO,m,y,V*" is authorised since it corresponds to phrases like *je m'y ferais*. The graph thus makes it possible to gather together and combine all authorised structures and enables the system to locate automatically their occurrence in texts. Figure 10 shows a sample of the result (62 occurrences) of a search on this grammar in the text of the script extract mentioned above.

95

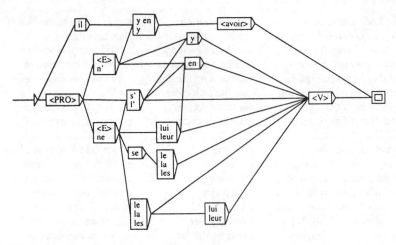

Figure 9 - pronoun order program

s jamais mis Non, une fois pour lui faire plaisir
fants, dépêchons-nous Eh dis donc ta mère comment
aux clients importants Vous mettrez celui en cuir
c'est à mon père, depuis qu'il a arrêté de fumer,
   Ah lui non plus ça a pas été le coup de foudre.
pouvait pas se blairer tous les deux J'espère qu'
ois c'est quand même plus marrant Mmm Tu crois qu'
ilà Papa ! à cause de toi, j'ai perdu, c'est vrai
lié les clefs à la maison T'en rates pas une toi
ensais Benjamin, il est 2 heures , va falloir que
a commencé à pointer le bout de son nez Bon ben,
l'avez dit Si papa, c'est vrai, tu l'as dit Bon,
ieur Ancelot. 36 rue Niepce, dans le quatorzième.
ça je te jure, c'est vrai, regarde Fais voir. Oh
pérables. Regarde ton jogging C'est pas grave, tu
uot appeler le commissariat tiens Où tu vas e Je
Dis! Faut que tu signes quand même Oh putain ! je
euh, si tu aimes pas les dessins de mon père, tu
puis trois jours maître Fournet S'il appelle vous
pa, c'est vrai, tu l'as dit Bon, je l'ai dit mais
re pour qu'ils soient comme ça ? A quoi ça sert ?
ois que ça m'arrive.Ben faites pas cette tête-là.
h, mon père il a rien compris au devoir de maths.
ouais, faut acheter un troisième steak A table !
n, finalement y avait personne. Mais heureusement
e doit dormir. Le samedi matin c'est toujours moi
qui fait courir les parents ? l'amour ! Qu'est-ce
vos conneries, j'ai oublié les clefs à la maison
in ? Mais non il est rien arrivé ! Qu'est-ce que
a petite. Il perdait sa chemise, alors ça je peux
evoir de maths. On y a passé tout le dimanche. Je
ivorcé. Il vit plus avec nous, alors. Bon, allez,
vrai Ah si, vous l'avez dit Si papa, c'est vrai,
e c'est que ce pyjama ? C'est ce cadeau de maman,
-là. Dulac ! Dulac ! d u l a c. Du - lac Celui-là
gez pas d'ici. Si les parents d'Olivia appellent,
our Benjamin Bonjour madame Je vais faire un jus,
û aller au commissariat Ben c'est pas vrai Ah si,
z changé de lunettes dites-moi Oh maître Fournet,
on. C'est vraiment très gentil de l'avoir gardée.
lot à l'appareil. Je suis le père du petit, enfin

ça lui a
elle l'a
en y ajoutant
il en mange
Il l'a
il leur faudra
il lui est
j'en étais
J'en rate
j'y aille
j'y vais
je l'ai
Je l'envoie
je le crois
m'en achèteras
m'en vais
m'y ferais
me le dis
me le faites
on l'a
on les changera
On les passera
On y a
On y est
qu'y avait
qui la réveille
qui les rend
T'en rates
t'en sais
te le dire
te le filerai
tu l'appelleras
tu l'as
tu l'avais
tu le connais
tu leur donnes
vous en voulez
vous l'avez
vous l'avez
Vous l'oubliez
vous le connaissez

fait plaisir ? Elle faisait la même tête que toi J
trouvé mon père ? Pas terrible Ah lui non plus ç
ma carte. C'est pour monsieur Ancelot. 36 rue N
tout le temps Ma mère aussi a arrêté de fumer. E
trouvée vachement coincée Remarque l'année dé
pas un an Cabinet Delambre-Chaligny, bonjour.
arrivé quelque chose ? Non, t'inquiètes pas Tu v
au septième niveau quoi ! Quoi ? eh eh c'est pas
pas une, mais qu'est-ce qu'on fait ? Qu'est-ce qu
! Tu m'écoutes ? Ouais, ouais Benjamin ! Et vo
. J'avais promis à Benjamin de faire vite, hein A
dit mais on l'a pas fait, hein ? maintenant avec v
par coursier ? Oui C'est facile à trouver ? parce
pas, comment t'as fait ? Ben tu vois, faut pas pre
un autre. T'étais où ? J'ai dû aller voir un clien
puisqu'on veut pas de moi ici Ben et ton beefste
jamais à ce nom-là. Dulac ! Dulac ! d u l a c. Du
hein, je le répèterai pas. C'est pas ça, mais je c
tout de suite savoir d'accord ? Bien sûr maître F
pas fait, hein ? maintenant avec vos conneries, j'
pas. L'amour ! Qu'est-ce qui fait, qui fait l'effe
à la javel, oh ! Non c'est pas la peine, merci ma
passé tout le dimanche. Je te le filerai à la récr
! Et voilà ! J'aurais dû acheter un boeuf ! Ben ja
Benjamin, on s'est vachement bien amusés tous
, alors, mais je veux pas aller au commissariat. S
complètement dingues ? l'amour ! Pourquoi tout
pas une toi J'en rate pas une, mais qu'est-ce qu'
? Et quand maman elle est entrée à la clinique ?
Heureusement qu'il était là, sinon Olivia passait
à la récré Tiens ça doit être à ton père. Ma mère
à la maison Ouais ! comme ça, tu pourras nous f
dit Bon, je l'ai dit mais on l'a pas fait, hein ?
jamais mis Non, une fois pour lui faire plaisir ça
? Non Il est super Mais tu sais euh, si tu aimes
bien l'adresse. Ouais. T'inquiètes. Tiens vas-y à
? Maman boit du thé le matin ça m'étonne pas. I
dit Si papa, c'est vrai, tu l'as dit Bon, je l'ai
remarqué ? Dites-moi Christine, vous qui savez
souvent ? Merde, j'ai plus de filtres dis donc. J'

Figure 10 - concordances corresponding to the pronoun program

96

Finding concordances may be linked to several different language teaching goals:

- support for class activities: pupils are able to observe and analyse linguistic phenomena 'in action' from concordances already prepared by the teacher, and then to formalise them (possibly in the form of programs).
- preparation of teaching materials: for example, teachers and designers can create exercise banks in which sentences corresponding to the targeted learning process are not 'invented' but taken from authentic utterances.
- precise evaluation of exposure to the language during the learning process (lexicon of simple and compound words, syntactic structures, frequencies etc.)

These high-level tools are intended for automatic processing of natural languages, but this does not make their introduction into teaching any less valuable. Contrary to certain generally accepted ideas, the most modest tools are not the best suited to educational uses.

References

Birckman, A. (1567). *Concordantiae*. éditions A. Birckman.

Courtois B., Silberztein M. (éd.) 1990. "Dictionnaires électroniques du français". *Langue Française* n° 87. Paris. Larousse.

Garrigues, M. (1993). "Prépositions et noms de pays et d'îles: une grammaire locale pour l'analyse automatique des textes". In *Lingvisticae Investigationes*. XVII: 2. Amsterdam. Philadelphie. John Benjamins.

Gross, M. (1989). "The use of finite automata in the lexical representation of natural language". In *Electronic Dictionaries and Automata in Computational Linguistics*, Berlin-New-York: Springer pp. 34-50.

Johns T.(1988). "Implications et applications des logiciels de concordances dans la salle de classe". In *Les langues modernes* n⁰ 5, 1988. "Le point sur l'EAO". APLV. Diff. Nathan. Paris.

Maurel, D. (1988). Grammaire des dates. Etude préliminaire à leur traitement automatique. *Lingvisticae Investigationes*. vol.12:1. Amsterdam. Philadelphie. John Benjamins.

Passelecq G., Poswick F. (1974). Table pastorale de la Bible. Index analytique et analogique. P. Lethilleux, éditeur. Paris.

Rézeau, J. (1988). "De l'utilisation d'un progiciel professionnel en E.A.O. des langues". In *Le français dans le monde*. Numéro spécial "Nouvelles technologies et apprentissage des langues". Août-Septembre 1988. Hachette. Paris.

Silberztein, M. (1993). *Dictionnaires électroniques et analyse automatique de textes. Le système INTEX*. Paris: Masson.

Software

The system *INTEX* is available from LADL, l'Université Paris 7 (2 place Jussieu, 75005 Paris). It runs under NEXSTEP (a Unix system available for 486 PCs).

MicroConcord: Oxford English software. Oxford University Press. 1993

7. DEALING WITH INFORMATION SYSTEMS. A TASK-BASED APPROACH
Yvan ROOSELEER - Belgium

1. Introduction

In many school subjects, including languages, we like to introduce real-life cases into the classroom. This article aims to describe possible ways of developing task-based activities in the context of a database system. *Tasks* are often considered as the basic block in a language curriculum. The term refers to a range of workplans that have the purpose of facilitating language learning. Tasks fit in well with the principle of communicative language learning, in which the learner is focused on meaning rather than on linguistic structure.

A database system contains useful language materials for didactic exploitation. A number of specific, task-oriented communicative skills can be trained in the context of a real-life database system. Many tasks engage the learners in activities like searching, understanding, managing, processing and transferring information in the target language. In this case, we consider the information found in a typical database system as the input data. As probably 90 % (or more) of all database systems worldwide are for business purposes, we will use a business database system as an example. This database will serve both for input and for output in many learner activities. For some tasks additional materials of different sources may be used.

The contents of the sample database lend themselves to quite a number of relevant communicative tasks. The *world* described in the database system will provide us with a realistic context in which the tasks can be situated. Typically, as most tasks involve more than one communicative skill, the skills are trained in an integrated way. Using a database system as an information resource is unfamiliar to many learners. Therefore we believe that, particularly in the initial stages, some tasks will need to focus the learner's attention on one or two skills to the exclusion of others. These will involve finding a specific piece of information required for some purpose in the database.

Many organisations rely on a database to support their daily operations. Throughout this article we will be referring to a sample database that is available in many different languages. Using an existing database can be a guarantee for authentic language.

The task-based approach we are proposing is similar to the approach in many textbooks and courses on language for specific purposes. We believe that the materials are equally suitable to be integrated as a topic in a general-purpose language course.

The target learner is obviously, but not exclusively, a business student with an interest in English for business or professional purposes. When most students will communicate in their professional lives, it may involve querying or updating a database. This information system will not necessarily be in their native language. In Belgium, a Dutch-speaking professional may have to deal with information systems in Dutch, French, English, German or any other language. So there is value in giving language learners some training in the use of database systems that are not in their native language.

Many of the tasks will directly appeal to the so-called "concrete learner", who may be a future salesperson, secretary or office clerk. Moreover, the problem-solving and hypothesis-testing activities that are possible in the context of this case study will especially appeal to the more analytic type of learner, who may be a future manager. The database contents can be adapted to the purposes of a specific target group. However, we think that adapting the activities to the target group is a more effective approach.

1.1 Prerequisites

1.1.1 *Target group*

- Language level: intermediate and above.
- Presupposed PC knowledge: word processing, databases, ...
- Restrictions: The students will not have to design a new database application.

1.1.2 *Teacher*

The teacher should be fairly familiar with business English. IT skills such as word processing are useful.

In order to prepare and manage classroom activities involving business information systems, the teacher should know how a database management system works. It may be a good idea to organise this as an integrated project involving teachers from different subject areas.

1.2 Task-sequence and presentation

The learning process will be organised in several stages. An initial exploration stage, in which the learner can find out more about the contents and structure of the database, is essential to build up confidence.

The tasks can be presented to the students in various ways:

- in writing, using worksheets or specially selected documents (e-mail messages, faxes, advertisements, business cards...) both on screen and on paper;
- orally, by the teacher, by co-students, in a role-play, via voice mail, via multimedia applications.

1.3 Classroom time

Between 4 and 20 (or more) hours of classroom activities are possible with the sample database, preferably in the form of a project with a lot of role-play activities and other types of interaction. For some activities additional materials may have to be prepared.

This case study integrates aspects of several school subject areas, notably languages, computer and business studies. It allows teachers from different subject areas to co-operate on a common project.

1.4 Other software

This case study does not limit itself to using database systems. As in a normal professional situation other software tools may be used in several tasks for transferring information into and out of the databases system: e.g. a word processor to prepare various sorts of messages (memos, letters, faxes, e-mail); a presentation package to prepare company or product presentations, ...

2. Database systems and communicative language learning

2.1 Language teaching methodology

A database system can serve as a resource for developing task-based learning materials. Several characteristics of language teaching methodology are involved.

Modular approach
Many language courses for general or specific purposes are modular. Units of work are organised around topics that reflect the needs of learners, general interest, or other content areas.

Authentic language
We want to use an authentic foreign language database system for learner input. This is important from a didactic point of view: if we want learners to comprehend oral and written language in the real world, then the learner needs opportunities for dealing with this real-world language in class.

Focus on meaning
The sample database contains interesting materials to create communicative tasks in a meaningful context that reflect the communicative needs of the learner. The language materials offer scope for a variety of communicative and problem-solving activities. Learner tasks will not only involve scanning for specific information, but also updating the database and adapting information from various (written or spoken) sources to a required format. The textual elements on-screen may be relatively small, but they still contain complete and meaningful messages. The database also contains some non-linguistic clues (pictures) which may make it more easy to arrive at meaning. In order for the tasks to be realistic, various other materials and resources can be used in addition to the database system.

101

Transactional and interactional language functions
Because a database system is a highly structured repository of information, many of the language functions are transactional. Even if transfer of information is central to the context of the sample database, some tasks also involve interactional language functions. Some of the information-gap activities enable both transactional and interactional language functions to be trained in a natural way.

Professional needs
Searching and updating (foreign-language) databases is a typical professional skill that can be trained with the aid of this sample database. Many tasks may also involve other typically professional skills like writing memos, faxes, reports, presenting information, telephoning, interpreting facts and figures, taking part in meetings and discussions, ... In those cases, the database serves as a resource to find the necessary information to accomplish the task.

Fluency/accuracy
Many of the proposed activities will involve both fluency and accuracy.

Top-down approach
Database systems normally use a top-down approach in managing information. Using a database for every-day business operations requires the learner to develop efficient top-down searching and reading strategies.

Word grouping
Research has shown that people remember words in groups which have something in common. As suggested by the schema theory, words should be studied in semantic networks. Word grouping activities can easily be developed in the sample database context, because the database uses a semantic approach, e.g. categories for products, for employees, ...

Information management
Tasks that result in association, categorisation, pattern learning and inferencing are easy to introduce in the context of a database system. A well-designed database system enables decision-making, so that the database system in fact becomes an *information management system.*

2.2 Computer use in the language classroom

There are many reasons for using computers in the language classroom. One approach uses computer technology to enhance language learning. The need for a PC arises from needs that come from within language learning. Traditional CALL, multimedia and telematics use computers for its surplus value as a learning tool.

Another approach uses computers for needs that arise from outside language learning. In this case study the learner is required to transfer information to and from a foreign language information system. The need for being capable of dealing with foreign language information systems comes from outside language learning, namely from professional needs.

3.   What is a database system?

Before describing the language materials and some possible classroom activities in greater detail, we think it is useful to give the reader some background information about database management systems. Databases have become essential for the day-to-day operation and competitiveness of many organisations, institutions and business companies.

Database systems represent the core of an information system and integrate all the relevant knowledge and facts. Finding a specific piece of information requires querying the database by using a top-down strategy. Obviously, those organisations mentioned above need people who can work in a database environment in an efficient way.

There are many links between linguistics/language teaching and database analysis and design. Key issues in both areas are *information management* and *knowledge of the world modelling*.

We don't think it is a good idea to teach database modelling in the language classroom. Nevertheless, integrating database systems into communicative language courses has many benefits because of the authentic language materials and the numerous opportunities for the learner to rehearse skills required in his later professional life. Other uses of databases are feasible for language learners, for example, vocabulary management.

3.1 PC databases versus large scale databases

Generally speaking, we can differentiate between PC-based (small scale) database systems and large scale systems. *MS Access* is a popular relational database management system developed by Microsoft Corporation for Windows PCs. Other well known PC database software include *Visual FoxPro* (also from Microsoft), *Paradox* and *Visual dBase* from Borland. The database systems mentioned above run on personal computers. On network platforms their performance is rather low because many users want to access and update the database at the same time. Therefore, on network systems large scale database management systems such as *Oracle, Sybase, DB2, SQL Server* and *Informix* are preferred as they can handle hundreds of transactions at the same time.

A PC-based database system is sufficient for the purposes described in this article.

3.2 Sample database

The database system referred to in this article is called *NorthWind Traders*. It comes as a free sample database with the *MS Access relational database system* and exists in many different languages. Because the data are in electronic format, the database contents can be adapted to various purposes.

MS Access is also a part of a popular application program suite, *Microsoft Office Professional*, made up of a number of application programs: a word processing program (*Word*), a spreadsheet program (*Excel*), a presentation program (*PowerPoint*) and a database program (*Access*). This text will focus on the database, but in many tasks the other applications may come in.

3.3 MS Access relational database management system for Windows

MS Access is a typical *relational* database system. Most of the things learned while using this software are transferable to other database systems. The terminology used in MS Access is similar to large scale database systems. Terms like *table, primary key, query, referential integrity, cascading delete, ...* are common.

Relational databases represent the dominant database technology of the 90's. Newer approaches based on object-oriented programming have begun to emerge. Most business database systems are so-called relational SQL databases. *Multimedia databases*, on the other hand, will most likely use object-oriented concepts.

The Access database menu contains the following typical choices: tables, queries, forms, reports, macros and modules.

Most of the time an average user will view the database information through forms and reports. Therefore many tasks in the language classroom will involve the use of forms and reports, rather than database tables, macros or modules. Some activities might require the student to make an ad-hoc query, especially when doing data analysis and problem-solving. The student should only use ad-hoc queries if he/she has had previous experience in a computer studies course.

3.4 Relational model

The *relational database model* is claimed to be a good formal model of certain aspects of the real world. Therefore a database is viewed as a model of a real-world situation. Many modelling techniques used for databases are based on *semantic modelling* because database systems typically have only a very limited understanding of what the data in the database actually means. For database developers, it would be nice if computer systems could understand a little more, so that they could respond a little more intelligently to user interactions. Semantic modelling is sometimes called *entity-relationship* or *top-down* modelling.

In designing a database, one tries to identify a set of semantic concepts that are useful in talking about the world. Some of the concepts that are used in *entity-relationship* (ER) modelling are listed in the following table.

Concept	Informal definition	Example
Entity	A distinguishable object.	Employee
Property	A piece of information that describes an entity. Clearly one entity can have several properties. Each kind of property draws its values from a corresponding value set or domain. Sometimes properties are called *attributes*.	Name, Age, Sex, Job description, Salary
Relationship	An entity that serves to interconnect two or more entities. A relationship can be one-to-one, one-to-many and many-to-many.	Employee E works in department D (1-1).
Subtype	Entity type Y is a subtype of entity type X if and only if every Y is necessarily an X. All properties of type X apply to type Y but the reverse is not true.	Sales engineer is a subtype of the Employee supertype.

The same object in the real world can be regarded as an entity by some people, a property by others, and a relationship by others. From one perspective, a marriage is clearly a relationship between two people (e.g. Who was Elizabeth Taylor married to in 1975?). From another perspective a marriage is clearly an entity in its own right (e.g. How many marriages have been performed in this church since April?).

A database consists of tables and columns: tables refer to entities and to relationships, columns refer to properties.

Several diagramming techniques are used to represent the semantic model, e.g. ER diagrams. Diagrams make it possible for non-technical people to understand the structure of a database.

4. Sample database description

The description of the sample database materials in the following paragraphs should give the reader an idea of the range of possible communicative classroom activities for foreign language learning.

4.1 NorthWind Traders

At the core of the classroom activities is a sample database called *NorthWind Traders*. We chose to use this database because it is readily available. It is included in a widely used commercial application program suite. We invite the reader to have a look at the real *NorthWind* database with the MS Access program (probably somewhere on a computer near you).

NorthWind Traders is a fictional firm with fictional employees and customers. They are wholesalers dealing in food and drink. Because NorthWind Traders are importers and exporters a multicultural approach is possible. In using this database for various communicative language learning activities, the learner's attention will be focused on meaning.

The database is central to the setting in which the tasks will be situated, for example, when preparing to write an e-mail message or a company presentation, the learner needs to query the database.

An important feature of the NorthWind Traders database is the authentic nature of the business situations and settings for the language work. The activities therefore will be relevant, challenging and motivating if pitched at the appropriate level. The database is suitable for both intermediate and advanced learners but the tasks and activities will vary.

4.2 Language

We are using the sample database "as is". The language materials are in an electronic format, so it is easy to adapt the materials to specific needs or purposes. It should be noted that a database, being in an electronic format, is dynamic: the contents can change as a result of actions by the learner.

The NorthWind database was not designed with language teaching in mind. It is a sample database for learning how to use a computer program. Most people working on this sample database will be native speakers who view it as a model for their own database system.

The sample database described here is in American English, but it exists in many different languages. We have seen versions in Dutch, French, English and German. Some translations rely heavily on the American model, but the teacher can easily insert new data to adapt the content to his or her own needs or purposes.

No doubt the (American) English language materials in the sample database are authentic. They are intended to be used by native speakers. Also the language is not too difficult so as not to distract native speakers wanting to learn new database skills.

4.3 Database contents

The database contains information about employees, products, customer orders, suppliers and shippers. The reader is advised to check out the NorthWind Traders sample database for more details.

5. Task components

5.1 Input

A lot of the information necessary to perform a task will come from the database. But not all the language input has to come from the database system. Various other resources can be used: order forms, invoices, catalogues, brochures, business cards, memos, e-mail messages, voice mail messages, passport photos, application forms, social security forms, curriculum vitae, letters, memo notes, drawings, economic graphs, timetables, ... The project involves input sources from subject areas other than foreign languages, notably computer and business studies.

5.2 Goals

Using a database system as a resource coincides with the objectives of many professional or business language courses. Such courses are intended to improve communication skills in meetings, discussions, presentations, telephoning, social contacts and the writing of short memos, faxes, e-mail messages, letters and reports.

A number of typical communicative skills and strategies (both general-purpose and specialised) can be trained in the context of the sample database:

-   The learner should be able to retrieve or obtain a specific fact or piece of information by scanning the database system in order to reply to a question (of a customer, a colleague, a supplier, ...). The initiating question and the reply can be written (*letter, fax, memo, e-mail, worksheet*) or spoken (*telephone, voice mail*).

-   The learner should be able to enter new information into the database system.

-   The learner should be able to transfer information from outside sources into the database system and vice versa. This will involve transforming information into the right database format.

-   The learner should be able to collect various pieces of information in order to make a decision (as in a role play or simulation).

To achieve many of the above mentioned goals, developing database-specific top-down (searching and reading) strategies will be essential.

This case study does not require the design of a new database system.

5.3 Activities

Many different activities are possible within the sample database context:

- Searching for a specific piece of information in the database (e.g. What job function ...? What product category ...? How many ... are in stock?);

- Searching for specific information for some given purpose, processing it and using it in some way (e.g. find out which customers have ordered a specific product that is discontinued and propose a replacement);

- Processing information or transferring information from the database to another format (e.g. draw a company structure chart and prepare a presentation about it; give a presentation commenting on the sales results from the last quarter);

- Updating the database system by transferring information collected from various sources to the required database format (e.g. fill in an on-screen employee form using personal biographical data; use a business card to fill in a new customer or supplier form);

- Information-gap interaction (e.g. complete missing parts in the database through exchange of information with a fellow student);

- Forecasting, predicting, inferencing (e.g. predict sales for the next quarter);

- Grouping and summarising (e.g. make a report of the sales of the last quarter, make a list of nationalities of customers and suppliers, make a list of all types of container found in the database);

- Solving problems by finding and processing information that will aid in making a decision (e.g. select a member of staff with the right profile to be a security officer);

- Solving problems through social interaction (e.g. search the database in order to prepare for a meeting that will decide on some business problem).

In computer science or in business studies classes the student might be engaged in similar activities. In the language classroom the focus will be on the learner's needs to find/process the information in order to communicate.

Databases are dynamic. As students perform specific tasks, objects and entities within the database system are bound to change. Many tasks involve updating the database. The learner is eventually responsible for the integrity of his personal database. When a learner has incomplete or incorrect information, he should try to get the required information through the help of another student, so that this will effectively be an information gap activity.

5.4 Setting

Most activities will be in a multimedia classroom set up as a workshop (networked PC's and communication equipment). Many activities will be small-group, since two or three students may be sitting at the same PC. For some tasks they will have to communicate with other small groups. A number of tasks may involve using tools such as electronic mail, word processing or presentation software. A lot of communication will be oral. The information from the database will be used as a means to train authentic communicative situations.

5.5 Roles

A suggested approach would be for the learner to have a specific role or job function within the NorthWind corporation described in the sample database. In the initial exploration stage, the learner could have a specific role or job function in mind.

Some role-plays will be unscripted, but other more complex situations (company presentation, products presentation, job application, sales meeting) will require preparation.

The teacher will act as a coach, an organiser and as a participant. There could be two (or more) teachers: one being a foreign languages teacher, the other being a computer science or economics teacher.

5.6 Topics

All topics of this case study are business-oriented, but we believe that the language materials are equally interesting for general-purpose language learning. The NorthWind database covers the following topics:

General: people, food and drink, countries, nationalities, place names, numbers, quantity, telephone numbers, postal codes, measurement and size, time, periods of time, dates, methods of communication;

Specific: buying and selling, trade and commerce, import and export, education, career opportunities and job positions, company structure, organisation chart, containers and packaging, money, price, price calculation, currency, discount, invoice, addresses, office terminology.

The NorthWind corporation of the sample database is an international organisation, which gives the database a strong multicultural flavour.

6. Learning sequence and strategies

6.1 Task sequence

In developing learner tasks we assume that the students already know how to use a database system like *MS Access* in their mother tongue.

Using a foreign-language computer database may be new for most learners. They should be given ample opportunity to explore the database. To do this in an efficient way we propose to prepare worksheets. The learners can work through the worksheets in pairs.

The worksheets aim at helping the learner to build up confidence in using a foreign language database system. A gradual increase in demands on the learner is the best approach. At the end of the exploration stage the learner should have developed a *'database attack'* strategy. Typically this will be top-down, because this is how a database system is designed.

At the end of the exploration stage the learner should be familiar with the database structure (tables, forms, reports, ...) and content (employees, job functions, product categories, products, customers, suppliers, markets, ...). He should know which on-screen form to choose in order to obtain certain information. He should also be able to decide if an ad-hoc query is necessary.

As soon as the exploration stage is over, learners can engage in activities that require transferring information from outside the database into the database system or vice versa. This is how database systems are used in real life. It may give the learner opportunities to work with different and varied authentic language materials: order forms, invoices, catalogues, brochures, memos, e-mail messages, voice mail messages, passport photos, social security forms, curriculum vitae, letters, memo notes, drawings, economic graphs, timetables, business cards, ...

Example task

A possible consolidation task at the end of the exploration stage would be the following:

- draw an organisation chart of NorthWind Traders;
- give a presentation about the company structure and target markets.

6.2 Language functions

The sample database provides a context for some specific types of language interaction: buying and selling, negotiating a sales agreement, giving or transferring information, answering enquiries, attending sales meetings, preparing product presentations, writing memos, faxes, e-mail messages, advertisements, letters of application, CVs, ...

The list of general language functions that can be practised is extensive: asking questions, making requests, describing, comparing, stating cause/effect relationships, future developments, forecasting, stating conditions, accepting or rejecting an offer, hypothetical statements, stating requirements, giving reasons, recommending and suggesting, persuading, talking about procedure, organising information, presenting information, information flow, ... Some language functions, and the related vocabulary and grammar, may have to be pretaught and trained before the task can be accomplished. In any case, the choice of task has to be adapted to the learner.

Some role plays will simulate real-life business situations, e.g. presentations, discussions or meetings. The database system will serve as the information provider for many of the role plays. Here is a list of language functions grouped according to types of interaction typical in professional situations:

- presentations: organisation, sequencing, referring to charts and tables;
- meetings: persuading, defending a point of view, criticising, arguing, summarising, agreeing and disagreeing, developing a point of view;
- discussions: exchanging information, advising, suggesting, insisting, ...);
- sending e-mail, faxing, telephoning: introducing oneself, arranging an appointment, requesting information, giving explanations, making complaints, giving apologies, etc.

6.3 Vocabulary

All communicative tasks involve using the vocabulary from the NorthWind database. Process materials for studying the new words will have to be prepared. We will suggest some possible preparatory activities. The sample database offers ample opportunities for activities involving word grouping and semantic fields.

6.3.1 *Human resources*

Here is a list of all the job functions occurring in the sample database:

Accounting Manager, Assistant Sales Representative, Marketing Assistant, Marketing Manager, Owner, Order Administrator, Sales Associate, Sales Manager, Purchasing Manager, Export Administrator. The database is easily expandable to contain more employees and different job functions.

Sample assignments

- Draw a word network of all the job functions in the sample database;
- A new receptionist has been recruited by NorthWind Traders. Enter all the relevant data for the employee that you can find using the following materials: letter of application, curriculum vitae, application form, notes taken during job interview, employment contract.

6.3.2 Product categories

Product categories appear in the database with a category description and some examples of brand names, showing that there definitely is a multicultural flavour.

Sample activities

- Match the descriptions on the left with the product categories on the right:

Breads, crackers, pasta, and cereal	Beverages
Desserts, candies, sweetbreads	Confections
Dried fruit and bean curd	Grains/Cereals
Seaweed and fish	Produce
Soft drinks, coffees, teas, beer, and ale	Seafood

- Find the product category of the following product brands:

  Steeleye Stout
  Ipoh Coffee
  Scottish Longbreads
  Vegie-spread
  Perth Pasties

- The database contains quite a number of funny brand-names. Invent new names for products to be added to the database.

- The sample database uses product categories to group products into categories. Create one or more product categories with a suitable description and enter a number of new products, e.g. pots, pans, plates, glasses, knives, forks, coffee makers, food processors, vacuum cleaners, feather dusters, aprons, brooms, ...

6.3.3 Containers

The products come in different types of unit or container:

Unit/Container	Example	Product example
Bag	100 - 250 g bags	Gumbär Gummibärchen
	20 bags x 4 pieces	Wimmers gute Semmelknödel
	50 bags x 30 sausgs.	Thüringer Rostbratwurst
Bar	12 - 100 g bars	Valkoinen suklaa
Bottle	750 cc per bottle	Chartreuse verte
	24 - 355 ml bottles	Outback Lager
	32 - 8 oz bottles	Louisiana Fiery Hot Pepper Sauce
Box	2 kg box	Konbu
	36 boxes	Chef Anton's Gumbo Mix
	10 boxes x 8 pieces	Scottish Longbreads

	30 gift boxes	Sir Rodney's Marmalade
	24 boxes x 2 pies	Pâté chinois
	10 boxes x 20 bags	Chai
Can	12 - 12 oz cans	Jack's New England Clam Chowder
	12 - 355 ml cans	Guaraná Fantástica
	25 - 825 g cans	Rössle Sauerkraut
Glass	10 - 200 g glasses	Nord-Ost Matjeshering
Jar	24 - 250 g jars	Inlagd Sill
	12 - 8 oz jars	Grandma's Boysenberry Spread
Package	16 kg pkg.	Carnarvon Tigers
	50 - 300 g pkgs.	Manjimup Dried Apples
Pie	48 pies	Tarte au sucre
Piece	100 - 100 g pieces	Schoggi Schokolade
	24 pieces	Escargots de Bourgogne
Round	15 - 300 g rounds	Camembert Pierrot
Tin	24 - 4 oz tins	Boston Crab Meat
	16 - 500 g tins	Ipoh Coffee

Sample exercise

-   What container is used for the following products ...?

    Boston Crab Meat
    Sir Rodney's Marmalade
    Grandma's Boysenberry Spread

6.4 Activity types

Several categories of tasks may be distinguished:

-   Comprehension questions (yes/no, multiple choice, ...);
-   Productive activities (complete a grid, ...);
-   Interactive tasks (information gap/simulation/discussion/problem-solving).

6.5 Comprehension questions

Many questions aim at locating information. At first the learner will be given the name of the form to be used in order to obtain a certain piece of information. Gradually the learner should be able to decide which form to use.

Many questions will involve finding a specific piece of information for a given purpose (name, age, price). Top-down reading and scanning will be the main strategies. The on-screen text is usually quite short, but deciding which form to use and spotting the required information is difficult enough.

Working in pairs with two learners sitting at one PC is a good approach as it will stimulate interactive language use.

113

6.6 Productive tasks

As opposed to the comprehension questions above, most tasks at this stage will involve more than searching for specific information; the learner will also process it and use it in some way.

Processing information from the database (e.g. how many ...?) involves making ad-hoc queries. The learner should for example be able to generate a list of distinct occurrences of a certain object (e.g. job functions, product categories, containers, ...) Many tasks involve combining, sorting or grouping information from the database. Database-specific search or query strategies may be required. Some tasks may be quite similar to those in a computer studies course.

At the end of the exploration stage a number of consolidation tasks should allow the learner to show that he understands the database structure and contents, e.g. draw company organisation chart, ...

Some task examples

- Using a business card and a company brochure fill out an on-screen form for a new customer.
- How many people are employed in the sales department of NorthWind? How many sales representatives are women?
- Add a new product or product category to the database with all the relevant data, using brochures, catalogues, ...
- You are in charge of sales at NorthWind Traders. Prepare a presentation of the sales results for each sales person.

- Make a list of all occurrences of ...

    - products that have been discontinued at NorthWind Traders;
    - product categories that are currently in stock at NorthWind Traders;
    - nationalities of customers;
    - nationalities of suppliers;
    - job functions of the contact persons in the customer table;
    - customers who regularly place an order (once a month);
    - customers who have not placed an order for three months;
    - suppliers from Italy;
    - containers and packaging of products.

114

6.7 Interactive tasks

6.7.1. *Information-gap activities*

These involve a transfer of given information from one person to another. The fact that learners do not have the same information will stimulate interactive language use between pairs of students. It has been shown that small-group, two-way information gap tasks are particularly appropriate for stimulating interactive language use. An information-gap activity, moreover, integrates all four communicative skills.

Information gap exercises that provide useful communicative practice, are easy to prepare. For example, all learners could have a different copy of the database with missing elements. The task consists of completing the personal copy of the database by asking co-students for missing names, dates, ... Several variants are possible:

- The learner is told what information is missing (e.g. all birth dates, ...).
- The learner is not told what information is missing and needs a strategy that helps him find missing information easily.

Some other possible assignments involving information gap

- Steve Buchanan, the sales manager from NorthWind Corporation, needs to know what type of packaging or containers are used for a number of products. Inform him by memo of the product category and the packaging used for the following list of products: Aniseed Syrup, Guaraná Fantástica, Ipoh Coffee, Jack's New England Clam Chowder, Scottish Longbreads, Sir Rodney's Marmalade, Steeleye Stout, Uncle Bob's Organic Dried Pears, Valkoinen suklaa.

- You received a fax from Lino Rodriguez from a firm based in Lisbon. He wants to find out what discount they would receive for the cheese product mentioned in their last order. If the discount is 15% or more, he wants to change the number of items ordered to 50 units. What kind of cheese have Rodriguez' firm ordered? What discount have they been granted? Reply.

- Maria Anders from Alfreds Futterkiste in Germany has lost some details of their most recent order. Look up the details of all the orders that were recently made. Send a listing of all products ordered by fax or e-mail. Use a word processor to prepare this document.

- Christina Berglund is order administrator for a business firm in Sweden. (Find out which firm.) She sent a fax enquiring about *Chef Anton's Cajun Seasoning*. She wants to order 20 units if the price per unit is below 30 GBP. Check the products database and find out if the price is acceptable. If there isn't enough in stock, place an order with the right supplier. (Find the supplier using the supplier database form.) Reply to Christina by fax. Prepare the fax using a word processor and find the correct fax number using the customer database form.

115

6.7.2   Reasoning-gap activities

These involve deriving new information from given information through processes of inference, deduction, practical reasoning, or a perception of relationships or patterns.

Some task examples involving reasoning gap activities (e.g. what course of action is best/cheapest/quickest ... for a given purpose and within given constraints?)

- Who is the best candidate for the new job of receptionist?
- NorthWind need to appoint an employee to take care of security problems. Who do you think has the best background? What criteria would you use? How would you find this person in the database?
- The Sales Manager is leaving NorthWind. Who do you think is the best candidate to take his place? Why?
- In which countries would you set up a subsidiary? Why? Who would start up the business?
- NorthWind Traders want to set up a number of business units (e.g. cheese products, wine, ...). If you were the manager of the business unit for cheese, what products would you like to import? How would you find suppliers?
- What new range of products do you think could expand the company?

6.7.3   Interactive problem-solving

Problem situations and scenarios can be developed which allow learners to rehearse real-world language while solving problems through social interaction with others. In the context of NorthWind the following are possible among many others:

- sales (import/export) negotiations in which the most *profitable* deal should be made;
- sales meetings where decisions are to be made;
- job applications where the most suitable candidate has to be selected.

7.   Conclusion

The language materials in the sample database are suitable for business and for general language learning purposes. Courses in language for business purposes will be able to fully exploit the didactic possibilities of the authentic materials and the communication opportunities. But language courses for general-purposes will also be able to use the materials as a learning module. There are many opportunities for rehearsal for the real world, using communicative skills that take into account both fluency and accuracy. The learner will also be able to develop confidence in working with foreign language database systems. The tasks require the students to use skills from different subject areas (languages, computer studies, business studies). Pedagogically this type of integration can be of great value.

116

The sample database is an interesting resource for developing learning materials for two types of learners: concrete learners and analytic learners. Concrete learners will like learning words and communication strategies in a real-life context. The references to 'real' people (picture, biography, job description) and actual 'brand-named' products will motivate them. Many of the communication activities will also appeal to them. The communicative tasks will often be transactional, but also interpersonal in many pair work and role play activities. Analytic learners will prefer the problem-solving, decision-making or hypothesis testing tasks.

We have listed a number of possible ways to use a database system as a resource and a learning environment. A database system offers the learner an environment in which to learn words and train language functions in a realistic context. By incorporating relevant tasks which relate to real-life communicative needs, the learner may be motivated to perform well. Many tasks involve training the four communicative language skills in an authentic setting and, very specifically, also aim at developing efficient top-down *database attack* strategies. Many tasks will involve searching for some specific information for a given purpose, processing it and using it in some way. Information-gap activities, which stimulate interactive language use, are easy to prepare. Various tasks engage the learners in problem-solving activities in which they are required to negotiate meaning. There are quite a range of possible activities, so learners can make certain choices in what, how and when to learn.

We have pointed out possible ways of integrating other application programs such as word processing, e-mail or presentation software into the tasks.

Using database systems in the language classroom may require the teacher to learn new *database* skills. Learning how database systems work is also worthwhile for language teaching purposes.

The computer has a central role in this case study, because most tasks cannot effectively be accomplished without a computer.

References

Date, C.J. (1995) *An Introduction to Database Systems*, 6th Edition, Addison Wesley.
Ellis, G. and Sinclair, B. (1989) *Learning to Learn English*, Cambridge University Press.
Goethals, M. (1995) *A European Multicultural Communicative Foreign Language Teaching Methodology*, in: Lies Sercu e.a., *Intercultural Competence: A New Challenge for Language Teachers and Trainers in Europe*, Aalborg University Press.
Lowyck, J. and Verloop N. (1995) *Onderwijskunde: een kennisbasis voor professionals*, Wolters Leuven.
Microsoft Office Professional (any version), Microsoft Corporation
Nunan, D. (1989) *Designing Tasks for the Communicative Classroom*, Cambridge Language Teaching Library.
Nunan, D. (1991) *Language Teaching Methodology*, Prentice Hall International.

8. TELEMATICS
Lis KORNUM - Denmark

Introduction

During the last decade an increasing number of language teachers have begun using electronic communication, hereafter referred to as "telematics", in the language classroom. For some, this practice developed naturally from the introduction of word processing to the writing process. For others, telematics provided the opportunity to contact teachers and learners in other countries with the ultimate aim of meeting these people during an exchange visit.

To me, the term telematics covers computer conferencing and database searching as well as electronic mail. With the recent development of Internet, in particular the World Wide Web, where the user can find, and download, educational software, sound, pictures and videoclips, it is becoming increasingly difficult to distinguish one category from another.

Another important change has been the disappearance of the different national and international electronic networks, with different standards, that formerly hosted various projects. The British educational network Campus 2000 still exists, but has opened access to Internet. A necessary step, but one which has resulted in the cancellation of most non-British users' subscriptions as they can now communicate with UK schools directly via Internet.

The French network, Missimix (formerly Sésame), closed in January 1995, and the projects accommodated there moved to Internet. In addition, with the correct software the Minitel-databases are now accessible from Internet.

With Internet as the common denominator, now is the time for all modern language teachers to take the opportunity to introduce telematics in their classrooms. But it is important to consider how much of the history of telematics during the last 10-15 years is relevant to today's users, as well as those in the future.

The battle between technology and pedagogy

This battle has been, and is still being, fought in all fields of Information Technology. In the case of telematics many projects never got off the ground because of technical difficulties, so there was no pedagogic content to discuss.

Many myths have been created around the use of telematics. Besides being complicated, even to computer scientists and technicians without training in electronic communication and standards, it was also said to be too expensive, at least for schools and other educational establishments. This myth still exists today, and it is true that one can accumulate a considerable telephone bill by surfing uncritically on Internet at all hours. However, as all "serious" users know, the transmission costs for a regular and methodological use of your electronic mailbox are negligible compared to other forms of communication.

However, many teachers have difficulties in making their authorities understand that if their institution is so lucky as to have a computer with a modem it does not have to be locked away in the Headmaster's office. More and more people are installing modems at home and communicating with their schools via their own computer and telephone connection. For some, it is the only solution if they want to communicate at all, while for others, like myself, it is simply much easier and therefore more tempting to do it from home. To a certain extent this practice is acceptable. Teachers have always done a large amount of their work at home, so why not continue? But if educational establishments come to rely on teachers doing all the extra work involved in a telematics project at home - and paying the transmission costs too - it might slow up the process of integrating telematics into the curriculum.

Fortunately, the explosive spread of the World Wide Web during the last year or two has put pressure on all kinds of institutions to improve the quality of the "information highway". Many establishments already offer extensive access to Internet to both staff and students. Society as a whole is experiencing a rapidly increasing demand from the public for easier and cheaper access to Internet. The public libraries have had difficulties meeting this demand, and numerous "computer-cafés" have sprung up within the last year or two, where anybody can walk in off the street and pay for half an hour's search on Internet. It is not just young people who are interested - a number of initiatives involving senior citizens have shown that this age group is also fascinated by the potential of this new medium.

Examples of projects involving telematics

Although the projects mentioned below faced problems which are now resolved due to technological progress, the pedagogic and didactic elements of these projects are still of interest. Projects arising from the Council of Europe "new-style" workshops 7[1] and 9[2] are described below.

---

[1] The theme of Workshops 7A and 7B was: *Using information and communication technologies in modern language teaching and learning in Europe* (cf. references at the end of this contribution).

[2] The theme of Workshops 9A and 9B was: *The use of new technologies in the learning and teaching of modern languages in vocationally oriented education [upper secondary (16-19) and adult education]* (cf. references at the end of this contribution).

a)   Workshop 7

At Workshop 7A in France in December 1991 the majority of participants wanted to work with telematics, and during the following two years many efforts were made to encourage people to subscribe to the same networks. This proved to be almost impossible, due to the different standards of the electronic networks, national interests, lack of support from the authorities etc. Still, the contacts established at Workshop 7A made people communicate by all available means, and gradually more participants obtained access to electronic networks, and several national networks opened access to Internet.

People began to send files by e-mail, rather than just sending an envelope with a disk. As Director of Studies, it was a great help to me, as I had to draft three reports with contributions from the participants. But the various working groups also started to exchange drafts by e-mail which were then continued by the other members. So much time was saved, because you could send your letter to many people at the same time, simply by adding their e-mail number to the message.

Deadlines were easier to keep, and several times e-mail actually saved a problematic situation, for example, when letters disappeared or faxes were mutilated, but could be reconstructed via the files sent by e-mail. So telematics was not only a theme for one of the sub-groups of Workshop 7, but also a tool that a great number of participants used in order to communicate.

Gradually, more teachers and classes started to communicate by e-mail, using either the British network Campus 2000 or the French network Sésame (later Missimix). Several of these electronic exchanges led to real exchange visits between students and teachers of different countries.

Another important subject for discussion at the workshop was the pedagogical exploitation of databases. For instance, some language teachers used news databases from the Minitel to construct grammatical exercises. Others used concordance programs in combination with databases, with interesting results. Other teachers used the contents of the databases as text material for ordinary classroom work or as the basis for e-mail exchanges or conferencing.

Some participants collaborated with teachers from another Council of Europe project in a project where four secondary schools used telecommunication to simulate business deals. The aims were to teach the students to work on an international level, to support the awareness and understanding of different cultural attitudes and to promote the skills of presentation, investigation and negotiation. The project consisted of 4 case studies - each school, in turn, taking the role of a seller, the other participants being the customers.

In general the communication between the classes involved the following:

1. First offer (collecting material, selecting and presenting, questionnaire, market research).
2. Response - possibly request for additional details.
3. Second offer containing necessary details.
4. Negotiations (prices, conditions, timing ...).
5. Settlement.

The cases were carried out successfully by means of fax and electronic mail: Campus, BT GOLD and Intermail (Austrian educational bulletin board). Although the students were highly motivated, the teachers had to invest a lot of time and effort to carry out the project, not least because of technical problems with the different networks.

This example shows that the borderline between vocational and general education does not have to be very distinct, and that both teachers and students can benefit from a collaboration between the systems.

b) **Workshop 9**

This point was also proved in Workshop 9, in which several of the participants from Workshop 7 also took part. The collaboration which continued in Workshop 9 proved to be extremely valuable, as people could benefit from the development of Internet/World Wide Web in the pedagogic and didactic methodologies that were developed in the course of the projects.

At Workshop 9A the telematics group split up into several sub-groups e.g. a) adult education; b) hotel and catering schools; c) environment; d) language learning for engineers.

After the workshop, many participants communicated regularly by all available means, particularly the hotel and catering schools and several visits were made to the partner countries. One of the current outcomes is the production by the Danish Hotel and Catering School of a CD-ROM, in several languages, which will be used to train students.

At Workshop 9B the telematics group merged with the group whose aims were to identify teachers' needs and to provide support for teachers. Their common ground was the belief that Internet will be a doorway into using IT for many language teachers. With this in mind, the group investigated a number of possible ways in which language teachers could exploit the possibilities of Internet.

Some of the main areas explored were:

- curriculum information/professional development;
- resources information (knowledge)/news (keeping up to date);
- communication/interaction (e-mail, conferencing);
- random access - discovery/exploration.

The participants continue their collaboration, mostly by e-mail, where information about new addresses on Internet, seminars, training courses etc. is circulated. Another positive development has been the increasing participation of countries from Central Europe, where technical and economic problems previously made collaboration difficult.

c)   Eurocall[1]

The desire to continue the collaboration begun in the two workshops has encouraged a number of participants to join EUROCALL, the European organisation for language teachers interested in information technology. EUROCALL, which now has its own educational database and a home-page on World Wide Web, organises a yearly conference, publishes journals and newsletters, offers help to organise workshops and so on. Language teachers from many different kinds of educational systems meet, both physically and electronically, to exchange experiences and ideas and to try out new materials. Recently language teachers from other parts of the world have started to participate in EUROCALL conferences and to invite EUROCALL members to take part in their own conferences and projects too.

d)   A Lingua Project in Action VB.

One of the offsprings of Workshop 7 was the establishment of a Lingua project in Action VB with the aim of developing new methodologies and new teaching material for foreign languages.

Four countries, Belgium, Greece, the UK and Denmark, participated in this project which was entitled "Telematique et didactique dans l'enseignement des langues". In the course of this project the participants developed a package of educational material in French in the form of a book containing four disks with various software and a video.[2]

From 1992-95, students and teachers from upper-secondary schools in the partner countries exchanged electronic mail regularly and organised teleconferences on a number of themes agreed upon in advance.

The project was greatly facilitated by the Danish-French telecommunication project "Petite Sirène", which gave many Danish French teachers a considerable knowledge of telematics. In this way the Danish group functioned as the driving force for the teachers from the partner countries, many of whom had little or no experience with IT

---

[1]   For more information about Eurocall contact: June Thompson, CTI Centre for Modern Languages, University of Hull, Hull HU6 7RX, UK. e-mail: Eurocall@uk.ac.hull World Wide Web: http://www.cti.hull.ac.uk/eurocall.htm.

[2]   For more information about this project contact the coordinating institution: FIPF (Fédération Internationale des Professeurs de Francais), CIEP, 1, Avenue Léon Journault, 92311 Sèvres,   France.   Coordinator: Lektor   Lis   Kornum,   e-mail:lis_kornum@fc.sdbs.dk

Inevitably, the partners encountered a number of technical difficulties. But considerable time and effort can also be attributed to differences in curricula, the teachers' working conditions, cultural background etc. The maintenance of deadlines is vital to all telematics projects and during the first two years technical or other problems often interfered negatively in several countries.

The Danish participants were located throughout Denmark, so most of our communication was done by e-mail from the beginning. Little by little, the other countries joined in, so that in the third and final year all the four partner countries communicated regularly by e-mail.

After a while, other countries asked to be allowed to take part in our teleconferences, so for the first two years I, as the coordinator, acted as a sort of human gateway and sent files from the French network, Missimix, on to Campus 2000 and Internet and vice versa. Together with the organisation EUROSESAME[1] the project established a gopher on Internet, and during the last year all communication, except with the UK, took place via Internet.

The main objective of the project was to improve the quality of e-mail exchanges. All electronic networks are filled with "junk mail" where young people exchange masses of futile information on pop-groups, sport stars etc. That is perfectly all right as a spare time interest, but numerous experiences show that students tire very quickly of this kind of communication in an educational situation.

In this project the partners tried to establish certain guidelines on how to run telematics projects. The traditional personal profiles were considerably shortened and instead the students were told to describe their country, the educational system, the political system etc. in their introductory letters. We tried to avoid the most trivial subjects and instead, for instance, studied the same literary texts, read articles about the same news item, or watched the same film and then discussed/interpreted them via telematics.

Several exchanges have taken place, both among the teachers and among the classes involved. The participants have been able to profit much more than usual from these meetings because the partners could prepare the trip jointly over the network in advance, and of course also exchange evaluations afterwards.

---

[1]   EUROSESAME is an international organisation for teachers interested in telematics. For further information contact: M Robert Valette, CIEP, 1, Avenue Léon Journault, 92311 Sèvres, France.

e) The European Studies Project, a Cross-Cultural Project[1]

In this project more than 250 schools, from general and vocational education, use telematics to debate current issues in various languages. There are two age-groups: 11-16 and 16-19, and the schools are arranged into clusters with schools from other countries. In many of the UK and Irish schools the co-ordinator is a history or geography teacher as the project is part of a subject called "European Studies", whereas most of the teachers from the other countries are language teachers.

The majority of communication is done by e-mail to ensure a rapid exchange of opinions, but the subjects are carefully chosen and well prepared by the students, so that both native speakers and language learners benefit from the exchange.

Besides the chosen topics many other things will be discussed, for example the Troubles in Northern Ireland, the peace negotiations in former Yugoslavia and Chirac's nuclear tests. The students often use their foreign partners as information sources, both about politics and literature. Last year my students took great pleasure in discussing with British students the novel Frankenstein compared to Branagh's film-version. They also discussed Macbeth and felt very comforted to know that Shakespeare is difficult for native speakers too.

Besides e-mail, a lot of snail-mail is circulated, including video and audio tapes, photographs, booklets, articles etc. An increasing number of schools have their own homepage on WWW with information about their school, the class, the area. This information is very useful if you are planning an exchange visit.

Pedagogical Advantages

a) Language Awareness

One of the main problems of traditional educational applications in foreign language teaching is that the communication between the teacher and the learner is artificial. It is a simulated rather than authentic communication, and often this reduces the learner to the level of an object for the programmed teaching process. Contrary to this, it should be emphasised that all good teaching must involve a real dialogue between teacher and learner - respecting both parties as active agents.

Bearing these observations in mind, telematics seems to be a very promising way to use information technology for educational purposes, particularly in foreign languages. Much language software has been designed simply to teach learners the most basic survival skills, instead of progressing to teach them some negotiating skills too. It is

---

[1]   For further information about the European Studies Project contact: Anne Fay, The European Studies Project, Ulster Folk and Transport Museum, 153 Bangor Road, Holywood, Co Down BT18 OEU, UK.

vital that IT applications for language learners do not focus only on beginners, but are applicable at all levels of language learning.

As an example, electronic mail need not only be used for communication between pen-pals but also for computer conferencing. The main objective is the content material of the message, and the learners are motivated because e-mail creates authentic and purposeful interaction situations in the classroom. There is a <u>real</u> receiver at the other end which forces learners to be responsible for their own productions.

The themes of such computer conferences are usually announced well in advance, so the participants have time to find relevant background material, which can be read and discussed in the classroom like any other material in the curriculum. The students can write in groups on the word processor and thus have time to structure language as well as contents, before the letters are gathered in one file and sent by electronic mail.

During the computer conference, which can last from a single day to several weeks, you can read the contributions from the other participants, either on the screen or printout. The students find this exciting, and my evaluations show a noticeable improvement in their <u>reading skills and language awareness</u>. This derives partly from the fact that they read the preparatory material very intensely because they have to tell the other participants about it, partly from reading a number of contributions in the target language as well from mother tongue speakers.

In their subsequent letters they will often start to use expressions and idioms, which they have assimilated from the other letters, resulting in a written language on a much higher level.

b)   **The Writing Process**

A common problem with group work in foreign language classes has often been to encourage the students to speak the target language in the groups. However, if they have to <u>produce</u> language on the computer screen, they are forced to <u>discuss</u> formulations at the same time as they discuss the contents. Writing contributions to computer conferences in groups, and about a theme which they have previously discussed orally, is an excellent way to overcome this deficit.

The fact that it is so easy to re-structure your writing on the word processor makes students write more freely and take more chances in their formulations. Furthermore, it allows the teacher to participate much earlier in the writing process instead of just correcting the final version at home. It goes without saying that the role of the teacher at this early stage of the writing process is that of consultant and not that of judge.

However, as a language teacher, it is wise to have a look at the students' letters before sending them by e-mail, in order to check a certain amount of linguistic correctness. Usually it is no problem - on the contrary - students are eager to show their work to the teacher, and experiences show that they actually use their teacher a lot in this process, both as a walking dictionary and grammar, if they are writing during one of the lessons, or to correct their first drafts, if they are writing on their own.

But it is no secret that the demand for linguistic correctness differs widely according to the different educational systems in Europe. Language teachers will have to teach their students how to distinguish among different writing styles in the foreign language(s). Themes planned a long time in advance, where every partner delivers a report to the others, demand quite a high degree of linguistic correctness, in order to do justice to the contents. By contrast, requests for information can be answered quickly, with the focus not on the language but on the information required. As with all other language teaching it is a question of finding the balance between helping the students to improve their language skills without killing their motivation and creativity.

When writing about the above-mentioned activities, I take it for granted that they are carried out off-line. In the first years of e-mail many people associated the term with something happening here and now, and I have participated in on-line chats with both my French and my English classes. Besides the increased costs and the practical difficulties of assembling everybody at the same time at the end of the line, I find the pedagogical outcome of these chats to be negligible, from a language teachers point of view. Fortunately the learners with whom I have worked, quickly became aware of this and preferred preparing their texts on the word processor where they had time to think.

However, a new area for communicating has opened up with the so-called MOOs (Multi Object Oriented) and MUDs (Multi User Domain) on Internet. In, for instance, Schmooze University (a virtual university), the user gets a plan of the buildings on the screen - the library, a classroom, the lecture hall etc. There you can meet other users engaged in various activities and discussions, and you can join in if you wish. Many serious educationalists regularly frequent these virtual meeting places, so for teachers this is an exciting new domain.

c)   **Intercultural Awareness**

In addition to helping the students with their linguistic correctness, an equally important function for the teacher is to discuss with the class the suitability of various discussion topics for different nationalities, for instance an Irish class when discussing abortion, a Belgian class when discussing AIDS, or a UK class when discussing racism.

Still, I have never found that I have had to exert censorship. Perhaps because the students themselves feel responsible for their product, and their language as well as their intercultural awareness is heightened by the stimulation, not a simulation, of communicating with real people.

Nevertheless, incidents from several international projects show that, even in European countries that apparently resemble each other, standards of political and moral correctness differ greatly as do the norms for linguistic correctness. When introducing telematics as a tool for students to use in the language classroom the teacher should simultaneously teach them "netiquette" i.e. correct behaviour on the net. Personally, I find this aspect of integrating telematics to be one of the most rewarding, because you can combine the teaching of language awareness with intercultural awareness.

In spite of the growing internationalisation in the educational systems, stereotypes are still thriving. Young people do not necessarily become more tolerant by spending their holidays abroad. On the contrary "personal, direct experience of another country or community and its different cultural realities does not, of itself, lead to acceptance of difference; it may increase existing tendencies of rejection and withdrawal into a familiar identity and culture", as it says in a recent Council of Europe publication.[1]

Consequently, it is a good idea to have "Stereotypes" as one of the obligatory themes in e-mail projects. In this way students can give vent to their prejudices under the pretext that they are only voicing the general opinion. An interesting feature is that they very often write about nationalities that are not taking part in the project - no doubt to be on the safe side. Ironical comments and descriptions about one's own nationality are popular, avoiding accusations of chauvinism. One of the main reasons is probably a certain shyness at the beginning of the electronic exchanges. Just as many students have to try jokes, not always very well translated, in their first letters.

As with the linguistic form of the students' letters, the teacher should discuss with the class why this particular description or joke could be offensive, and try to persuade them that this is not a constructive way to communicate. Because this is an <u>authentic</u> situation where the receiver is a real person who could be hurt, the students learn that combining language awareness with cultural awareness is not only useful but necessary.

While the pedagogical advantages of electronic mail are praise-worthy, it must be admitted that a major problem has been to find partners who were willing and able to communicate regularly. Even if a school managed to conquer the technical and economical difficulties, they still had to find a suitable partner. Most people want to use a foreign language and then have the replies from mother tongue speakers, which of course is an ideal learning situation.

However, sometimes the mother tongue speakers insist on only sending questionnaires to their foreign partners in order to collate statistics on young people's (ab)use of alcohol, tobacco and drugs, or on how much they watch television, practice sports etc. In such cases, the different aims and objectives between foreign language teaching and teaching social sciences, geography or history in the mother tongue are clearly noticeable. The foreign language students are disappointed by the sterile way of communicating, and seen from a language point of view, they get nothing out of answering such questionnaires. One solution is to ask the mother tongue teacher/students if the foreigners can write an essay instead, where they try to respond to the questions of their partners. To base statistics on the replies of randomly chosen foreign students is academically and scientifically risky, but such projects can succeed, if all partners agree on the terms.

---

[1]   From *Young people facing difference*, Council of Europe Publishing, 1995.

In the first years of telematics the smaller countries and languages were less popular partners. Fortunately, this situation is now changing as, for instance, British and French schools begin to realise that a French school may perfectly well communicate in English with a Dutch school. The interest in exchange visits to countries with less widespread languages has also increased, in many cases because the inhabitants are known to speak foreign languages well.

For example, many Nordic countries have started exchanges with Italy, Portugal, and Greece during recent years and have used English, French and German when planning the exchange by e-mail.

Exploiting databases

When consulting databases the practice of working off-line as much as possible can also be recommended. Not only to avoid high transmission costs - many institutions have already solved this problem with more or less free access to Internet - but just as much to have time to study the material carefully, before you decide to use it.

Off-line communication can be almost as fast as on-line, and just as satisfactory, if not more so, to the learners, as I will try to show by the following example:

Before the French referendum on the Maastricht Treaty I consulted French databases like Agence France Presse, Libération, Le Monde etc. with my French class. We downloaded the bases quickly onto a disc. The class received printouts of the most interesting news to study at home for their next French-lesson, the day after the French referendum. That morning we again consulted the French databases - the class took turns looking at the screen while I downloaded, and the rest wrote letters on the word processor to send out on the network. We had a lesson of two hours, after which I sent out all their letters. We received the first reactions the same afternoon.

I find that the students' language awareness is sharpened by such teaching methods, and the fact that they can compare the language of databases and the "paper"-newspapers makes them notice the different ways language is used in the media. As one of the students said, " Mitterand speaks just like a database." Which was true of his speech on the evening of the referendum, but certainly not true of other of his speeches, which I then had to show them.

Besides news, another important use is library databases where students and teachers can find information about which books to consult for major assignments and exams. In most countries this access is cheap, if not free, and the libraries will even send you the relevant articles or books, if you e-mail them your address.

CD-ROM or Internet?

Much of the same material is to be found on CD-ROMs, many of which are updated several times a year. The price of CD-ROMs, as well as of the equipment, is steadily falling, so the last years have seen a rapidly increasing use of this tool in education. Its limitation is of course that, like a book, it cannot be updated, but a new copy must be made. This has led the IT-guru Negroponte to pronounce the CD-ROM dead in his latest book "Being Digital".

All information must now be found on Internet!

I agree, if one is looking for topical information or news, but in the case of established literature or art, I still find the CD-ROM very useful. I know that one can visit the Louvre Museum on Internet, but even with good connections the pictures take a very long time to appear on your screen, contrary to the CD-ROM (price FF 390) from the Louvre where you can study a great number of the finest works in detail, get comments, historical background etc. - quickly and without further costs.

On the other hand, I quite understand that more and more young artists form organisations that put their works on Internet, in order to become known by a larger public.

Media Awareness

The amount of information of all kinds that can be found on either Internet or CD-ROMs increases every day. This usually occurs without any rules as to correctness, credibility, language or structure. As a teacher it is impossible to know all the possibilities available, even within one's own subject area. So what can be done to make sure language teachers and learners exploit these fascinating facilities without "getting lost in Cyberspace"?

The debate has already started and censorship is being exerted on Internet with peculiar results. One well-known example is that the word "breast" was judged too sexy for the Net, which, among other things, caused the elimination of a whole computer conference/newsgroup discussion on breast cancer!

Are people easier to manipulate because the medium uses new and advanced technology which might shift our focus from content to form?

How can teachers check whether the information a student has found on Internet is correct? What rules and regulations should be set down concerning the use of quotations and references from Internet in academic publications, if the source is not well-known from other media?

One of the advantages of the new technologies is that they can bring authentic and topical material into the classroom and thus inform the learners about both the culture and the language they are trying to learn. An important task for the teacher is then to integrate the different tutoring or support material into a didactic framework. Teachers must assist learners in managing and structuring the mass of information they have access to. By adopting the role of consultant and facilitator they can help the learners to become active participants in their own learning, rather than passive consumers.

130

Distance Teaching and Learning

The fast evolution of society - the changes in technology, economy, culture - will increase the demands for education and training. The traditional educational institutions are unable to manage these demands exclusively by traditional means, the main problem being that the channels which we normally use to pass on new information and knowledge will turn out to be insufficient. For that reason telematics, and distance teaching and learning, will be an important educational tool.

In the past, we have seen much educational software of varying quality and success. Furthermore, we have noticed how these applications reflect different pedagogical concepts and methods progressing from simple instructions to experimental software designed to appeal to the creativity of the learner.

The number of distance teaching and learning projects is rapidly increasing, so I have chosen a case story to illustrate a model which has been successful:

A commercial college organising modern language teaching as distance education.

During the past 4 years the Southern Denmark Business School has developed and carried through a distance learning project. In fact it is no longer a "project" but an established part of the educational programme of the college. The courses mentioned are called "Studies for the specialised Language Diploma" - and they have been developed for English, German and French. The target group of the courses is multilingual secretaries, who want to supplement their expertise through in-service training. The duration of the courses is 2 years (half time studies).

The background for the development of the new courses is:

- The commercial colleges would like to enrol more students in this field;
- The trades and industries require highly qualified translators;
- The multilingual secretaries need qualifications, but they are very busy and want flexibility built into the courses.

In response, the Southern Denmark Business School started to work out a concept for courses partly based on telecommunications. Essential to the success of the courses was very careful planning and teacher training. From the start the team of teachers took part in course development and decision making. The teachers realised that they were employing a new medium, and that they had to develop a new way of teaching. A new curriculum was designed for distance learning and new teaching materials - compendia, books and electronic materials - were produced.

The courses have been structured by means of modules representing the following subjects:

- Interpretation and texts	(1 module)
- Terminology and databases	(1 module)
- Economy and social studies	(1 module)
- Commercial law and legal language	(2 modules)
- Technical language	(2 modules)

The students and the teachers see each other once a month for a whole day. In between these face to face meetings, they will be studying their books and compendia and communicating through computer conferencing. The conferences are used for very different kinds of communication: questions, good advice, translation drills, comments, discussions, references, chats etc.- not unlike a real class room. A large number of students have already completed the courses, and in their evaluations they stress the following benefits of distance education:-

- Flexibility - students can study at work or at home, at a time which suits them;
- Few fixed meetings;
- The knowledge of fellow students and teachers is always available;
- Students can always review old conversations, discussions, instructions and advice in the conferences;
- High quality of the compendia.

The teachers feel that they have to overcome some difficulties, when they teach at a distance:

- The teachers must work hard as "pacers" in the conferences in order to initiate, inspire or provoke discussions;
- The teachers must learn how to exploit the possibilities of individualised teaching but also how to set limits.

However the teachers also see important advantages:

- Flexibility. Students may work mostly at home;
- Teaching materials are ready when students start - or easy to revise;
- Standardisation and re-use of electronic texts (instruction, guidance, corrections).

Several European educational institutions, associations and companies have experienced the possibilities of distance education within the past few years: Commercial colleges, Open Universities, The Trade Unions, Teacher Training Colleges etc.

Even though distance education has turned out to be a success in some of these fields, it is important to realise that this kind of education cannot and should not be used at all levels of foreign language teaching! For instance, the physical presence of the teacher will still be necessary in primary and secondary schools. However telecommunications and some techniques from distance learning could very well be integrated in the traditional way of teaching.

Examples:

-   *Contact with experts*
    If you are working on a poetry workshop in a class, it would be useful to be able to contact a professional writer via Internet for inspiration and guidance. In the same way you might integrate a nuclear physicist as a kind of electronic guest teacher in a course on nuclear energy.

-   *Exchange of teachers* (small and well-defined electronic courses)
    If an English teacher is working on the fall of the Berlin Wall in his/her German lessons, he/she might be able to use a German colleague from Berlin as an electronic guest teacher. In exchange the English teacher could offer to be a guest teacher for the German class on the theme "Belfast". This type of exchange would indeed promote interdisciplinary co-operation in the schools.

Distance Teacher Training

The use of telematics for distance education will certainly make demands on the teachers. New teaching methodologies, curricula, compendia, books, and electronic materials must be developed.

To achieve this goal the teachers need an updated and efficient INSET training. Much of what was taught at teacher training courses just 2-3 years ago is now obsolete, and has been replaced by new requirements. With distance teacher training it will be possible to extend the courses, so that teachers and participants are electronically connected before, in between and after the face to face sessions.

In many countries language teachers have opened electronic conferences on their national networks, which could be expanded to become international electronic "conferences" for questions, discussions, exchange of ideas and exchange of materials, such as study plans, literature, glossaries and notes. Internet already offers a wide range of conferences, but what are required are more specific educational conferences where current topics could be debated by those genuinely interested in a particular field.

Journals and reviews will still be necessary for longer, in-depth articles. But more and more teachers are using electronic bulletin boards and conferences to disseminate, or request information about educational material, seminars, useful addresses etc. Instead of waiting several months until the journal is published and distributed, you may get an answer the next day which could solve your problem.

Systematic international collaboration is needed in order to benefit from such possibilities. Several projects mentioned in this chapter have shown that it is possible to train language teachers from different countries to use telematics in their classes within a reasonable timescale. The new EU-actions and projects from the Council of Europe can contribute to such a pan-European collaboration thus avoiding purely national initiatives which duplicate each other.

Conclusion

It is vital that telematics, and in particular distance teaching and learning, is not used in such a way as to make the learner feel isolated as frequently depicted in cartoons of "the lonely learner" in the media. Teachers also need the face to face contact with colleagues at regular intervals. The same applies to student exchanges. Telematics is an excellent tool for teaching and learning foreign languages, and a valuable support for face to face encounters which, besides the expense, can be difficult to integrate into the curriculum. However, nothing can ever replace human contact.

Telematics represents a challenge to the creativity of foreign language teaching. New strategies and techniques in language learning and teaching have to be developed, and judging from my experiences most language teachers are now willing to integrate new technologies into their methodology. With the necessary in-service training, foreign language teachers will be able to add an inspiring and important dimension to more traditional classroom practices.

References

Audits Linguistiques et Analyses des besoins, Actes du Symposium, Saarbrücken 1994, Bureau Lingua, Bruxelles.
Byram, M. and Zarate, G. (1995) *Young people facing difference* Strasbourg, Council of Europe.
Foreign Language Learning and the Use of New Technologies, conference proceedings, London 1993, Bureau Lingua and Delta, Bruxelles.
Fox, J. (ed.) (1992) *New Perspectives in Modern Language Learning,* a.o. University of East Anglia.
Kohn, J./Wolff, D. (eds.) (1994) *Neue Methoden im Fremdsprachenunterricht* Szombathely.
Lær og skriv, Gymnasieafdelingen, Undervisningsministeriet, Danmark, 1994.
Pogner, K.-H. (ed.) (1994) *More about Writing*, No. 6, Odense Universitet, Danmark.
Report on Workshop 7A. *Using information and communication technologies in modern language teaching and learning in Europe.* Sèvres (France) December 1991. Compiled and edited by M. Garrigues.
Report on Workshop 9A.. *The use of new technologies in the learning and teaching of modern languages in vocationally oriented education [upper secondary (16-19) and adult education].* Grimstad (Norway), September 1992. Doc. CC-LANG (92). Compiled and edited by A.-K. Korsvold.
Sheils, J., (1993) *Communication in the modern languages classroom*, Strasbourg, Council of Europe.
SIRENE-Projektet, Ny Informationsteknologi i franskundervisningen i Gymnasiet. Undervisningsministeriet, Danmark, 1994.
Télématique et didactique des langues, ed. the Lingua Project in Action VB, 1995. FIPF, CIEP, 1, Avenue Léon Journault, 92311 Sèvres, France.

8. TEACHER DEVELOPMENT FOR THE USE OF INFORMATION TECHNOLOGY

Erich ZEHNDER - Germany

Introduction

For more than just technological reasons, teachers need to reflect the changing roles of the learning partners in the language learning process. It is often said that future teachers can no longer afford to be the master at the centre of traditional instruction learning scenarios. Quite the contrary, teachers need to regard their function more and more in terms of moderating re-organised and adaptive learning environments. They should consider their role as that of providers and managers of learning opportunities enriched by the use of increasingly flexible learning materials and resources.

Learners also need to assume a more active role in learning. They should not just function as simple communicators or receivers of tuition. Their role as experimenters and researchers, autonomous task-finders and decision takers, needs to be developed by learning scenarios such as project-based, task-based and content-oriented learning. Such an approach is very much in line with current concepts of learning-oriented and learner-centred approaches to language learning and acquisition which promote learner autonomy and "learning to learn".

The new communication and information technologies are both complex and expensive. Hard- and software development are moving so quickly that the average language teacher sometimes sees more difficulties than advantages when attempting to make effective use of these new tools in language learning. However, the ability to make use of IT tools and resources will be one of the basic skills future teachers will have to acquire as part of their training. As a result, the issue of teacher training and new technology was also discussed in the course of the new-style workshops referred to in this compendium. Apart from the need for a technology related component in initial training, various aspects of in-service training were researched and tested by one of the R & D project groups at Workshop 9. This paper briefly summarises the topic, while further information can be obtained from a brochure and an accompanying video produced by the group, which document the results and the various pilot seminars conducted as part of the project.

Getting started

At the Council of Europe Workshop 9A at Grimstad in 1992 on "The use of new technologies in the learning and teaching of modern languages in vocationally oriented education [upper secondary (16-19) and adult education]" a group of four started the research and development programme "Development of Teacher Training Module(s) on the Use of Information Technology (IT) in Vocationally Oriented Language Learning".

135

The group designed teacher-training seminars and piloted them in various countries several times. The result of this piloting and its evaluation provides basis for the description of the teacher training modules in this article. The video tape demonstrating different parts of the module was produced with the support of the institution of one of the group members from Austria - the Verband Wiener Volksbildung.

Software criteria

Considerations concerning software should take into account the cognitive and emotional aspects of human cognition. The choice of appropriate software should, therefore, be based on the following criteria:

- Software that supports the learning of a foreign language should offer opportunities for interaction with the language.
- Any software used should engage the learner in experimental and explorative learning.
- The learner should be in charge of his own learning progression.
- Open software is important because it gives ample opportunities to support the knowledge and skills necessary to start the learning processes.

It is also clear that software should be user-friendly in terms of being able to give sufficient feedback to the learner, so that the computer functions as an acceptable tool for the learner.

Hardware criteria

Any software is useless if the hardware is not adequate to run it. Therefore, certain criteria should also be applied to ensure that suitable hardware is chosen (PC/compatible or MAC). Initially, one should be familiar with the various functions and technical specifications of the hard disk. The next step is to check whether the hardware is suitable for the user's purposes, and what purposes the computer will serve (single working stations, server, network). When choosing a printer, it is equally important to specify which functions will be required. There is no sense in investing large amounts of money in a fancy printer with a multitude of options, such as colour printing and paper management, if you do not need these facilities.

Organisation of in-service training on the use of modern technology in language teaching

It is important to bear in mind the necessity for a logical progression in teacher training modules. The basics relating to didactics and methods in computer assisted language learning should be the focal point throughout the training. Equally important are comprehensive demonstrations of the applications of soft- and hardware. By paying attention to both the limitations and possibilities of the computers and software used, participants may be given a chance of acting as exploratory learners themselves, especially through hands-on sessions after any demonstration. An important aspect at this stage, is to support and reassure the participants with follow-up training and

136

encouragement in the face of demotivation or problems that might occur while working with the new tools.

The context of training should be carefully considered also, bearing in mind the computer literacy of participants. It is important that participants try to overcome any "technophobia" from which they suffer: an atmosphere of trust and comfort is necessary before moving into the world of computers. The teacher trainers should be careful not to present themselves as a computer "gurus" but rather emphasise their position as primarily "computer illiterate" language teachers. Possibly negative effects on the less experienced participant/teacher should never be underestimated! Teacher trainers should carefully explain all the necessary technical terms, in order to familiarise the participants with the new vocabulary.

Furthermore it is vital to relate all presentations and discussion to didactics and each teacher's everyday work situation. If this is maintained as a fundamental principle throughout the training course, the chances of winning more enthusiasts for this approach increase remarkably. Thus the training will not be something imposed on the individual teacher, but rather be an eye-opener to how his or her work in the classroom may be improved. Most important of all: the individual teacher will enter a process where his or her proficiency as a teacher will be the basis for further choices to be made. The participant/teacher will be empowered in terms of how, where, when and why he or she will make use of computer programs in the teaching process.

Target groups of the in-service training

As indicated above, it is necessary to carefully consider the target group of the in-service training in order to achieve the best possible results. Training should have the emphasis directed towards the vocational aspect, and in this context the definition of the target group is essential. Having defined the target group, it is possible to choose the most effective methods of teacher training. Seldom is one confronted with a homogenous group of participants, but it is quite possible to get an over-all impression of the target group by asking questions such as: What is the history of previous in-service training? Is there a recognisable pattern? What expectations, if any, do the future participants have? Are there any prejudices about the subject (technophobia), any particular (personal) difficulties that become obvious? Is the target group familiar with concepts such as "communicative language learning", "explorative learning", etc.?

One of the most important aspects of this pre-training preparation is to define the target group sufficiently, in order to be able to plan everything according to the particular target group. A sensitive approach to the target group, in terms of letting the participants introduce themselves and their expectations to the group before commencing, will help the training itself, and build confidence, not only between the training group and the teacher trainer, but also within the group itself. This process will, in turn, help prevent group conflicts, but implies a high degree of awareness on the part of the teacher trainer.

A certain knowledge of group dynamics will undoubtedly help the teacher trainer understand and support the learning process of his or her participants throughout all training sessions. The real training situation must be constantly adapted to the one already pre-planned to ensure the best learning conditions. Various personal relations within the group may hinder or strengthen the training situation, and should therefore be carefully monitored. It is equally important not to speed up the progression of the training if participants show signs of not being able to follow the original training design. This situation may also occur because of a technical breakdown. During hands-on sessions it is possible to help individual participants and thus individualise the training, but it is equally important to keep the group together while instructing and lecturing. The role of the instructor / lecturer / trainer should be the same as in any other language-learning classroom. Dealing with a fairly heterogenous training group does not necessarily cause more problems, but definitely increases the pedagogical challenge.

Awareness of the group's weaknesses and strengths will help the trainer choose the right path and speed for the training. An informal evaluation at the end of each session will also be of great help in this respect. The participants should be encouraged to freely air their opinions, both orally, and in written form at the end of the course. This kind of evaluation will be highly valuable in the final judging of the effectiveness of the whole training course.

Descriptions of modules

The following explanations and descriptions are meant as suggestions as to how one might present hardware and software for language learning purposes. It is important to introduce the various possibilities step by step, as the participants' skills improve.

General views on the matter

The increasing demand for in-service training and life-long-learning, where foreign language teachers also need input to improve and modernise their classroom situation, will call for CALL (= Computer Assisted Language Learning) in the future. Language teachers need to prepare themselves for this reason. The concept of new technologies in language learning takes into consideration that most teachers of foreign languages have little or no experience at all in the use of computers:

Module 0:   General introduction to the subject, where no previous experience of IT in VOLL (Vocationally Oriented Language Learning) is presumed.

Module 1:   Presentation of concordancing and authoring programs suitable for one's own teaching material preparation.

Module 2:   Software which is meant for the classroom.

138

Details of the Modules

Module O

This so-called "motivation module" should introduce the participants to the subject in general. It is important to include a sequence on language-learning theory, methods and didactics in order to show the various perspectives. This approach will help improve awareness of the strengths and shortcomings of CALL programs. In this respect it is of vital importance that the trainer specifies:

1. Why computers may be used.
2. When and how software may be used in the teaching process.
3. Which program to choose in a particular classroom setting.

It is particularly important to consider the criteria by which software should be chosen in order to initiate and serve the language learning process:

- possibilities of interaction;
- experimenting and/or exploration;
- supporting and confirming the process.

Assuming that language learning strategies are part of the mental "software" of human beings, the key must be to make use of computers and programs compatible to our own cognition. Apart from software criteria, an introduction to software in general should be added at this stage. Different kinds of software offer different kinds of possibilities. Software should be presented in categories representing various aspects of language learning. This will help the participant/teacher gain an overview of the software available.

Module 1

At this stage, participants can get acquainted with certain programs which they can use in their actual language teaching process. Concordancers and authoring programs are the most important software in this respect. WIDA and authoring programs are tailored for specific language learning activities, such as STORYBOARD, PINPOINT, MATCHMASTER, TESTMASTER, CHOICEMASTER and WORDSTORE. The concordancing programs are of equal importance. They make use of authentic texts, which is a great advantage when dealing with language learning for specific purposes. Any document fed into the program will serve as a basis for the search for certain words or structures.

There are many programs available which produce gap exercises and vocabulary exercises. They are produced for limited purposes and should be taken into consideration, simply because learners do not necessarily need complex programs when practising certain basics of language. One main aim should be to understand the utility of a certain program for the learner at a particular stage in his or her language learning process. It is also important to carefully consider what to expect from a particular software in the preparation phase, and whether it is user-friendly, for teacher and learner. The following are a few factors to consider:

- target-oriented;
- motivational possibilities;
- the use of colour, graphics, animation etc.;
- facility to change from the main program to others;
- easily accessible help functions;
- both target-oriented and flexible sequence training;
- continuous feedback or evaluation available etc.

Apart from the above mentioned criteria, there are other aspects to be considered. These depend on which categories of programs and computers are available:

- general hardware specifications and compatibility;
- speed of loading, input and answer;
- possibilities of interaction between the learner and the program;
- variations in exercises through repetition;
- variety of exercises in terms of form and questions;
- facility to individualise the program.

Such data and considerations will facilitate making the right choice when exposed to the descriptions of computers and programs in manuals.

Module 2

At this stage, the actual use of computers in the classroom is the issue. Multimedia products are particularly interesting in this respect. They combine traditional software with sound and sometimes animation which make these products particularly attractive and motivational for learners.

Conclusion on the modules

As mentioned earlier, both informal and formal evaluation by the participants is very important. The informal feedback might help the trainer adjust the course during its progress. It also ensures that the actual output of the course is evaluated by the participants. Evaluation may be in the form of an interview or a questionnaire, or simply by having the participants write down their personal views anonymously. There might be a "third party" engaged for the purpose of observing the training, looking for certain specified objectives or giving a general evaluation of the whole learning process. In any case, there should be some sort of evaluation taking place in order to improve the next session(s).

General conclusions and perspectives

It is essential to keep in mind the purpose of the teacher training. The use of computers should be a tool to improve the actual teaching of a foreign language, both in terms of preparation and of classroom work. The modular approach also ensures that computers are made available for all language teachers without any previous knowledge, or computer literacy. The level of efficiency of the training course will increase with homogenous groups, but should not be the main goal for training in general. Some participants will only attend the introductory module, but having participated in it, there should be a fair understanding of the subject, and in turn, an acceptance of the tools used by their colleagues.

At all three stages the following uses of the programs should be emphasised:

- the use of computers to prepare a lesson
  (preparation of worksheets, collection of texts, etc.);
- the use of computers in the classroom for presentations and group work;
- the use of computers by individual students in the classroom;
- the use of computers on a self-access basis or at the students' homes.

Clearly, teacher development must not neglect issues such as motivation and confidence. It is important to realise that both of these feelings are based on a sound sense of competence. Continuous updating of skills, as well as personal development and training for the individual teacher are important elements of any language learning programme. This teacher training concept, developed by an international group of teacher trainers in three different countries, is intended as a starting point for the development of further modules. A teacher training module for Business English has already been created. No doubt further modules will follow.

CONCLUSION
Anne-Karin KORSVOLD and Bernd RÜSCHOFF

As can be seen from the contributions to this compendium, the activities of the different R & D groups at Workshops 7 and 9 generated a wide variety of useful and interesting products. Yet, it was not just "product orientation" which made this series so successful. The interest and dedication of all those involved in the projects between the workshops was just as much concerned with initiating and developing human and professional links with colleagues working in different environments. The excitement of being engaged in pioneering activities, combining the latest information technologies with well-tried language teaching practice, was sustained and a number of activities were continued even after the "new-style" workshops had been completed.

Obviously, the editors do not intend to repeat what has already been discussed in detail by the contributors to the compendium. However, a few of the key issues on the subject of IT and technological resources in language learning discussed in this publication need to be summarised. As far as language learning methodology is concerned, the limitations and restrictions of learning scenarios with a purely communicative or instructivist bias have become more and more evident. In consequence, cognitive constructivist scenarios for language learning, embedded in a post-communicative language classroom focusing on more authentic forms of learning in the context of task-based, project-based and process-oriented learning, appear to be sound pedagogical principles upon which concepts of designing and exploiting any type of technology enhanced resource for language learning could be built.

It must be noted, however that the real contribution to innovation in language learning lies in the tool-function of IT and Technology Enhanced Language Learning (TELL) resources. Research has shown that even the use of straight-forward word processors can enhance the acquisition of writing and text comprehension and processing skills. This is particularly true when other "real-world" tools are integrated into word processing packages, such as thesauri, grammar and vocabulary checkers and tools for putting together multimedia and hypertext presentations. Learning scenarios based on project work resulting in electronic dossiers in a hypertext format can greatly enhance strategic (learning) knowledge and competences in information processing and knowledge construction. Data bases and CD-ROM resources in the form of subject related or general knowledge encyclopaedia are equally beneficial to the learning process. In addition, software for setting up individual or classroom related databases, such as classroom dictionaries or curriculum-related encyclopaedia, can be good (cognitive) tools for learners as well. Finally, concordancing tools are perfect for putting learners in a position where they can discover forms and structures or patterns of meaning and principles of word formation on the basis of their own research.

Lastly, telecommunication is developing into a global platform which will be of tremendous help when language learning attempts to go beyond the restrictions of isolated classrooms, thus overcoming some of the limitations of a communicative approach in such a traditional organisation of learning. Access to global information networks, communication with native and non-native peers or tutors, teleco-operative project work which transcends the confines of the traditional classroom and the use of telematics in distance learning are just a few of the possibilities the INTERNET and the World Wide Web have to offer to language learning.

With these considerations in mind, participants and contributors at "new-style" Workshops 7 and 9 drew up recommendations, which can be summarised as follows:

1. Information and Communication Technologies and their multimedia applications should be integral parts of all modern language curricula. They provide teachers and learners with authentic materials and cultural information and help to promote intercultural awareness and mutual understanding. They should be embedded in a principled and harmonious approach to language teaching, taking the interests and the learning styles of young people as their point of departure.

2. Since Information and Communication Technologies facilitate international contacts between teachers and learners, all educational establishments should have access to communication networks so that teachers and learners can fully exploit the educational potential of modern technology.

3. The use of Information and Communication Technologies for distance learning, both at a national and international level, should be promoted in order to make educational provision more flexible and accessible to a wide range of users. This is especially relevant for language learning in a vocational context.

4. The key to the introduction and acceptance of Information and Communication Technologies lies in teacher development. Information about and training in appropriate use of modern technologies as well as handling of the necessary technical equipment is essential. Access to technical support should be open to all teachers of modern languages. Furthermore, initial and in-service teacher training programmes should induce teachers to integrate such media into their daily classroom practice and professional life.

5. The Council of Europe should examine possibilities for, and foster continued co-operation between, colleagues involved in the development of Information and Communication Technologies and their pedagogical application in its member States. The Council of Europe should therefore further the establishment of a forum/bulletin board and a database. It should also encourage the formation and strengthening of special interest groups within existing networks devoted to promoting foreign language learning.

In summary, it should be noted that the majority of the project groups at the Council of Europe new-style Workshops dealing with new technologies concurred that traditional

144

scenarios of CBT (Computer Based Training) do not take real advantage of the full potential of IT for foreign language learning. It appears that the role of IT as provider of learning and teaching resources and tools for both learners and teachers corresponds better with the pedagogical and methodological principles which are emerging in a post-communicative era of foreign language learning. Such a tools-based approach together with the exploitation of both local and global resources is very much in line with current innovative approaches in foreign language learning methodology.

As far as basing the exploitation of IT resources in language learning on sound pedagogical and methodological principles is concerned, an important point to be stressed once again at the end of this compendium is the fact that the integration of any IT resource into a language curriculum must be firmly based on an "informatique pedagogique utilitaire." (Pelfrêne, 1986). This means that IT tools and resources must not confront learners with traditional "drill and kill" exercises and comprehension tests but rather with tools to enhance the acquisition of language processing and language production strategies and competences.

If such systems are well designed and the relevant concepts for their application are well thought out, the use of IT in language learning can provide both teachers and learners with powerful facilities to handle a number of the tasks involved in the learning and teaching of a foreign language more effectively: effective not simply in the sense of solving a given task, but in the sense of adding to learning scenarios in which the interactive construction of new knowledge and the acquisition of skills and strategies are of equal importance. As far as hypermedia are concerned, "... the transformation of knowledge ... is the litmus test we should use in judging both exploratory and constructive hypertexts." Such tools engage "... learners in looking at material in new ways" (Jackson, 1988, p. 12), thus drawing on and hopefully restructuring and adding to their knowledge base.

In this context we see the potential of the hopefully not too brave new world of IT enhanced language learning: powerful tools that are available not just to facilitate task handling but to facilitate the application and acquisition of strategies of language processing and language production in a learning to learn environment. In this way, Information Technology and TELL resources might actually be the perfect tool to assist the transition from instructivist learning scenarios towards a more constructivist paradigm of language learning.

BIBLIOGRAPHY

The following bibliography is intended a as brief reference for those readers who want to look further into the fields touched upon in this volume.

Reports on Council of Europe international workshops related to the theme:
(available in the language indicated by the title; 7B is a combination of English and French).

Rapport de l'Atelier 7A. *Moyens technologiques de l'information et de la communication au service de l'enseignement/apprentissage des langues vivantes en Europe.* Sèvres (France) décembre 1991. Doc. CC-LANG (92). Coordonné par M. Garrigues.

Report on Workshop 7B/Rapport de l'Atelier 7B. *Using information and communication technologies in modern language teaching and learning in Europe/Moyens technologiques de l'information et de la communication au service de l'enseignement/apprentissage des langues vivantes en Europe.* Gillelje (Denmark/Danemark) April/avril 1994. Doc. CC-LANG (95). Compiled and edited by/coordonné par L. Kornum.

Report on Workshop 9A.. *The use of new technologies in the learning and teaching of modern languages in vocationally oriented education [upper secondary (16-19) and adult education].* Grimstad (Norway), September 1992. Doc. CC-LANG (92). Compiled and edited by A.-K. Korsvold.

Report on Workshop 9B. *The use of new technologies in the learning and teaching of modern languages in vocationally oriented education [upper secondary (16-19) and adult education]*[1] Karlsruhe (Germany), April 1995. Doc. CC-LANG (95). Compiled and edited by B. Rüschoff.

Council of Europe Publications:

Girard, D. & Trim, J.L.M. (eds.) (1988). *Project No. 12: Learning and teaching modern languages for communication: Final report of the Project Group (activities 1982-87).* Strasbourg: Council of Europe.

Holec, H. (1988). *Autonomy and self-directed learning: present fields of application.* Strasbourg: Council of Europe.

Trim, J.L.M. (1988). *Council of Europe Project No. 12: Learning and teaching modern languages for communication - Consolidated report on the programme of international workshops for trainers of teachers of modern languages 1984-87.* Strasbourg: Council of Europe.

---

[1]   Moro, B. 'Hypermedia software applications: from content oriented to to methodology oriented design'. In this report.

Bibliographies and software guides

CTI Centre for Modern Languages (Ed.) (1990): *Software Guide*. Issue No.2, August 1990. Hull: University of Hull, Centre for Modern Languages.

European Commission: Bureau Lingua/DELTA (1993) *Foreign language learning and the use of new technologies: conference proceedings*, Brussels: EC.

Eastment, D. (1994) "CD-ROM: an overview of available materials", *Modern English Teacher* 3, 4: pp. 68-77.

Jung, U.O.H./Lieber, G.(1993): *An International Bibliography of Computer Assisted Language Learning with Annotations in German* (Vol.2). Frankfurt a.M.: Verlag Peter Lang.

Jung, U.O.H. (1988): *An International Bibliography of Computer Assisted Language Learning with Annotations in German*. Frankfurt a.M.: Verlag Peter Lang.

Jung, U.O.H. (1986): "Computer und Sprachunterricht. Eine teilkommentierte Auswahlbibliographie", *Die Neueren Sprachen* 85, pp. 185-212.

ReCALL Software Guide No. 3 (1993). University of Hull, CTI Centre for Modern Languages.

Other publications

Ahmad, K. (u.a.) (1985): *Computers, Language Learning and Language Teaching*. Cambridge: Cambridge University Press.

Ambron, S./Hooper, K. (1990): *Learning with Interactive Multimedia*. Redmont, Washington: Microsoft Press.

Baldry, A. (1990): *Research into Self-Access Study for Advanced Learners: Computer-Assisted Studies of English*. Udine: Companotto Editore.

Barlow, M. (1987): *Working with Computers: Computers Orientation for Foreign Students*. La Jolla, California: Athelstan Press.

Barnett, L. (1993). "Teacher off: Computer technology, guidance and self-access". *System*, Vol 21, No 3, pp. 295-304.

Bates, P.J. (u.a.) (Ed.) (1995): *Telematics for Flexible and Distance Learning (DELTA) - Final Report*. Brussels: Commission of the European Communities, Directorate-General for Telecommunications, Information Market and Exploitation of Research (DG XII).

Baumgartner, P./Hall, A. (Ed.) (1991): *Language Learning with Computers: An Educational Challenge*. Klagenfurt: WISL.

Bee-Lay, S./Yee-Ping, S. (1991): "English by e-mail: creating a global clasroom via the medium of computer technology". *ELT Journal* 45 (4), pp. 287-292.

Brierley, W./Kemble, R.I. (Ed.) (1991): *Computers as a Tool in Language Learning*. Chichester: Ellis Horwood.

Brücher, K.H. (1991): "Autorenprogramme im computergestützten Fremdsprachenunterricht". *Deutsch als Fremdsprache* 3, pp. 175-180.

Brumfit, C.J. (ed.) (1985): *Computers in English Language Teaching: A View from the Classroom. ELT Documents* 122. Oxford: Pergamon.

Burgess, G.J.A. (1990): "Time for evaluation, time for change: CALL past, present and future". *Computer Assisted Language Learning* 1, pp. 11-18.

Burgess, G.J.A. (1992): "The invisible machine - the context of hypertext". *Computer Assisted Language Learning* 5 (3), pp. 129-137.

Butler, J. (1990): "Concordancing, teaching and error analysis: some applications and a case study". *System* 18 (3), pp. 343-349.

Cameron, K.C. (1989): *Computer Assisted Language Learning*. Program structure and principles. Oxford: Blackwell Scientific Publications.

Carpenter, P./Egloff, G./Watters, E. (ed.) (1994): *Basic Communicative Skills & Cultural Knowledge of Transnational Vocational Placements*. Léargas: PETRA Ireland Coordination Unit.

Catt, C. (1991): "CALL authoring programs and vocabulary development exercises". *Computer Assisted Language Learning* 4 (3), pp. 131-139.

Challe, O. (1991): "Les spécificités d'un média moderne: la télématique". *Les Langues Modernes* 85 (1), pp. 59-68

Chesters, G. (Ed.) (1987): *The Use of Computers in the Teaching of Language and Languages*. Bath: CTI Support Services, pp. 127-138.

Cook, V.J. (1985): "Bridging the gap between computers and language teaching". *ESL Documents* 122.

Courtois, Bl. & Silberztein, M. (1990): "Dictionnaires électroniques du francais". In: *Langue Francaise* No. 87. Paris: Larousse.

Crosby, M.E. (u.a.) (1994): "Hypermedia as a facilitator for retention: A case study using Kanji City". *Computer Assisted Language Learning* 7 (1), pp. 3-13.

Daniel-Vatonne, M.-C. (1990): "Hypertextes: des principes communs et des variations". *Les Hypertextes - Technique et Science Informatiques* 9 (6), pp. 475-492.

Davies, G. (1991): "Expodisc - an interactive videodisc package for learners of Spanish". In: Savolainen, H./Telenius, J. (ed.): *EUROCALL 1991 - International Conference on Computer Assisted Language Learning - Proceedings*. Helsinki: The Helsinki School of Economics and Business Administration, pp. 133-139.

Davies, G. (1985): *Using Computers in Language Learning: a Teacher's Guide*. London: Centre for Information on Language Teaching and Research.

Davies, G. D., Bangs, P. & Betts, F. (1994) *Investigation into the use of language training materials in SMEs with a special focus on those incorporating new technologies: study on Lingua Action III projects*, Brussels: Lingua Bureau, Commission of the European Communities.

Debyser, F. (1989): "Télématiques et enseignement du français". *Langue Française* 83, pp. 14-31.

Dietberger, A: (u.a.) (1995): "Einige Fragen zur Entwicklung von Hypertext-Autorenwerkzeugen". *Informatik Forum* 9 (1).

Donaldson, R.P. (u.a.) (1994): "Reading is creative, too! A discussion of two hypercard stacks which can facilitate second-language reading comprehension". *Computer Assisted Language Learning* 7 (3), pp. 195-208.

Donath, R. (1991): "Telekommunikation im Englischunterricht". *Praxis des Neusprachlichen Unterrichts* 38 (2), pp. 161-169.

Eastment, D. (1996) "The Internet for teachers and learners", *Modern English Teacher* 5, 2: pp. 58-82.

Eck, A./Legenhausen, L./Wolff, D. (1995): *Telekommunikation und Fremdsprachenunterricht*. Bochum: AKS Verlag.

149

Farrington, B. (1994): "BonAccord revisited". *Computers & Education* 23(1/2), pp. 21-26.

Farrington, B. (1986): "Computer assisted learning or computer inhibited acquisition?". In: Cameron, K (u.a.) (ed.): *Computers and Modern Language Studies*. Chichester: Ellis Horwood, pp. 85-92.

Fox, J. (1989): "Can computers aid vocabulary learning?". Cameron, K.C. (ed.): *Computer Assisted Language Learning*. Program structures and principles. Oxford: Blackwell Scientific Publications, pp. 1-13.

Fox, J. (u.a.) (1992): *New Perspectives in Modern Language Learning*. Moorfoot: Learning Methods Branch, Employment Dept.

Garrigues, M. (ed.) (1988): *Nouvelles Technologies et Apprentissage des Langues* (Numéro spécial de Le Français dans le Monde - août-septembre). Paris: Hachette.

Gillespie, J./Gray, G. (1992): "Hypercard and the development of translation and vocabulary skills". *Computer Assisted Language Learning* 5 (1-2), pp. 3-11.

Girard, D. (ed.) (1992): *Actes des Etats Généraux des Langues: Technologies de la Communication*. Paris: Hachette.

Goodfellow, R. (1995): "A review of the types of CALL programs for vocabulary instruction". *Computer Assisted Language Learning* 8 (2-3), pp. 205-226.

Goodfellow, R. (1994): "Design principles for computer-aided vocabulary learning". *Computers & Education* 23(1/2), pp. 53-62.

Guillot M.-N., (1993): "Computer information systems and learner independence - a word of caution". *ReCALL*, issue No 8, pp. 16-20.

Guillot, M.-N-/Kenning, M.-M. (1994): "Electronic monolingual dictionaries as language learning aids: a case study". *Computers & Education* 23(1/2), pp. 63-73.

Günther, A. (ed.) (1994): *Computerbasiertes Training und Fernlernen*. Berlin: Köster.

Hainline, D. (ed.) (1987): New Developments in Computer-Assisted Language Learning.London: Croom Helm.

Hassert, Timm (1990) *Software für den computerunterstützten DAF-Unterricht*. München, GOETHE-Institut.

Higgins, J. (1991): "Which concordancer? A comparative review of MS DOS software". *System* 19 (1/2), pp. 91-99.

Higgins, J. (1988): *Language, Learners and Computers: Human Intelligence and Artificial Unintelligence*. London: Longman.

Higgins, J. (1988): *Language Learners and Computers*. Harlow: Longman.

Higgins, J./Johns, T. (1984): *Computers in Language Learning*. London: Croom Helm.

Holzmann, C./Peters, K. (ed.) (1991): *CALL Austria Nr 15 - Sondernummer Man And The Media*. Wien: CALL Austria.

Hubbard, P. (1992): "A methodological framework for CALL courseware software development". In: Pennington and Stevens (ed.): *Computers in Applied Linguistics: An International Perspective*. Clevedon: Multilingual Matters, pp. 39-65.

Hubbard, P.L. (1987): "Language teaching approaches, the evaluation of CALL software, and design implications". In: Smith, W.F. (ed.): *Modern Media in Foreign Language Education*. Lincolnwood (IL): National Textbook Company, pp. 227-254.

Jackson, M.J. (1988): "Siren Shapes: Exploratory and Constructive Hypertexts". In: *Academic Computing*, November, pp. 10-42.

Janssen, J./van Loon, H. (ed.) (1991): *New Media in the Humanities*. Selected papers from the International Conference on interactive audio, interactive video and open learning 24 and 25 October 1990. Amsterdam: University of Amsterdam.

Johansson, S./Stenström, A.-B. (ed.) (1991): *English Computer Corpora: Selected Papers and Research Guide*. Berlin: Mouton de Gruyter.

Johns, T. (1991): "Data-driven learning and the revival of grammar". In: Savolainen, H./Telenius, J. (ed.): *EUROCALL 1991 - International Conference on Computer Assisted Language Learning - Proceedings*. Helsinki: The Helsinki School of Economics and Business Administration, pp. 21-22.

Johns, T. (1991): "From printout to handout: Grammar and vocabulary teaching in the context of data-driven learning". In: Johns, T./King, P. (ed.): *ELR Journal Vol 4: Classroom Concordancing*. Birmingham: University of Birmingham.

Johns, T. & King, P. (eds.) (1991) *Classroom concordancing*, Special Issue of the *ELR* Journal 4, University of Birmingham: Centre for English Language Studies.

Jones, C./Fortescue, S. (1987): *Using Computers in the Language Classroom*. Harlow: Longman.

Jung, U.O.H. (ed.) (1988): *Computers in Applied Linguistics and Language Teaching*. Frankfurt a.M.: Verlag Peter Lang.

Kenning, M.-M./Guillot, M.-N. (1994): "Le Robert Electronique: A reassessment of the case for dictionary-based work". *Computer Assisted Language Learning* 7 (3), pp. 209-225.

Kenning, M.-M./Kenning, M.J. (1990): *Computers and Language Learning: Current Theory and Practice*. New York (u.a.): Ellis Horwood.

Kleinschrot, R. (1993): *Sprachen lernen mit dem Computer*. Reinbek bei Hamburg: Rowohlt.

Kornum, L. (1993): "From foreign languages methodology point of view". *Foreign Language Learning and the Use of New Technologies*. Brussels: Bureau LINGUA/DELTA, pp. 32-39.

Kornum, L. (1993): "Foreign language teaching and learning in a multimedia environment". *CALICO Journal* 10 (3).

Kornum, L. (1991): "A multimedia learning environment - experiences and evaluation". In: Savolainen, H./Telenius, J. (ed.): EUROCALL 1991 - International Conference on Computer Assisted Language Learning - Proceedings. Helsinki: The Helsinki School of Economics and Business Administration, pp. 182-190.

Krüger-Thielmann, K. (1991): *Wissensbasierte Sprachlernsysteme*. Neue Möglichkeiten für den computergestützten Sprachunterricht. München, Universität München: Centrum für Informations- und Sprachverarbeitung.

Lam, F.S./Pennington, M.C. (1995): "The computer vs. the pen: A comparative study of word processing in a Hong Kong secondary classroom". *Computer Assisted Language Learning* 8 (1), pp. 75-92.

Laurillard, D. (1993) *Program design principles*, Hull: TELL Consortium, CTI Centre for Modern Languages, University of Hull.

Legenhausen, L./Wolff, D. (1992): "STORYBOARD and communicative language learning: Results of the Düsseldorf CALL project". In: Swartz, M.L./Yazdani, M. (ed.): Intelligent Tutoring Systems for Foreign Language Learning: The Bridge to International Communication. Berlin: Springer, pp. 9-24. (s.a.9.2.4 u.9.2.6).

Leech, G./Candlin, C.N. (ed.) (1986): *Computers in English Language Teaching and Research*. Harlow: Longman.

Levy, M. (1996) *CALL: context and conceptualisation*, Oxford: Oxford University Press.

Levy, M./Farrugia, D. (1988): *Computers in Language Teaching*. Footscray: Footscray College of Technical & Further Education.

Little, D. (1994): "Interactive videocassette for self-access: a preliminary report on the implementation of Autotutor II". *Computers in Education* 23.1/2, pp. 165–70.

Little, D. (1988): "The Autotutor. An interactive videocassette system for language learners". In: Jung, U.O.H. (ed.): *Computers in Applied Linguistics and Language Teaching: A CALL Handbook*. Frankfurt a.M.: Lang, pp. 71-77.

Meinhof, U.H./Bergman, M. (1991): "Interactive video as a tool for text comprehension. An experiment with television news". In: Janssen, J./van Loon, H. (ed.): *New Media in the Humanities*. Amsterdam: Institute of Applied Linguistics, pp. 55-65.

Meinhof, H.U. (1990): "Television news, the computer and foreign language learning". In: Anivan, S. (ed.): *Language Teaching Methodology for the Nineties*. Singapore: RELC Anthology Series 24, pp. 250-263.

Meskill, C. (1991): "Language learning strategies advice: a study on the effects of online messaging". System 19 (3), pp. 277-287.

Monteith, M. (ed.) (1993): *Computers and Language*. Oxford: Intellect Books.

Motteram, G.J. (1990): "Using a standard authoring package to teach effective reading skills". *System* 18 (1), pp. 15-21.

Murison-Bowie, S. (1993): "Concordancing corner - what is concordancing and why should we do it?". In: *CALL & TELL* 4, pp. 42-44.

Murray, Denise E. (1995): *Knowledge Machines: language and information in a technological society*. London: Longman.

Niedersächsisches Kultusministerium (ed.) (1989): *Neue Technologien und Allgemeinbildung, Band 6: Englisch. Anregungen für den Unterricht*. Hannover: Berenberg.

Nielsen, J. (1990): *Hypertext & Hypermedia*. London: Academic Press.

Pelfrêne, A. (1986): "Lecticiel". In: *Triangle* 6, 135-142.

Pennington, M.C. (ed.) (1989): *Teaching Languages with Computers: The State of the Art*. La Jolla, California: Athelstan Press.

Pennington, M.C. & Stevens (ed.) (1992): *Computers in Applied Linguistics: An International Perspective*. Clevedon: Multilingual Matters.

152

Peters, K. (1991): "Interactive video - a new medium for applied language teaching".
In: Holzmann, C./Peters, K. (ed.): *CALL Austria Nr 15 - Sondernummer Man
And The Media*. Wien CALL Austria, pp. 158-170.

Rautenhaus, H. (u.a.) (ed.) (1993): "Telekommunikation im Englischunterricht".
Reihe *Oldenburger Vordrucke* der Carl von Ossietzky-Universität.

Rebensburg, K. (1994): "Fernlernen mit Kommunikationsdiensten". In: Günther, A.
(ed.): *Computerbasiertes Training und Fernlernen*. Berlin: Köster, pp. 21-44.

Reeves, N./Wright, C. (1996): *Linguistic Auditing*. A Guide to Identifying Foreign
Language Communication Needs in Corporations. Clevedon: Multilingual
Matters.

Reichl, F. (u.a.) (1995): "Support of distance learners by tutored media instruction".
Informatik Forum 9 (1).

Rézeau, J. (1994): "Integrating telematics data into CALL packages". *Computers &
Education* 23(1/2), pp. 159-164.

Rézeau, J. (1991): "Minitel and Framework: towards a global learning environment".
In: Janssen, J./van Loon, H. (ed.): *New Media in the Humanities*. Amsterdam:
Institute of Applied Linguistics.

Richmond, I.M. (1994): "Doing it backwards: Using translation software to teach
target-language grammaticality". *Computer Assisted Language Learning* 7 (1),
pp. 65-78.

Romiszowski, A.J. (1990): *Developing Auto-Instructional Materials*. London: Kogan
Page.

Rüschoff, B. (1996): "Technology Enhanced Resources and Information Technology
in Language Learning". In: *Language Teaching* (in print).

Rüschoff, B. (1995): "Freies Lernen für freie Lerner? - Neue Formen der
Kommunikation und des Lernens per Datenautobahn und
Informationstechnologien". *Computer und Unterricht* 18.

Rüschoff, B. (1995): "Technologiegestützte Lernsysteme und Datenbanken und
Untersuchungen zu Spracherwerbs- und Sprachverstehensstrategien". *Die
Neueren Sprachen* 94 (5).

Rüschoff, B. (1993): "Language learning and information technology: state of the
art". *CALICO Journal* 10 (3).

Rüschoff, B. (1988): *Fremdsprachenunterricht mit computergestützten Materialien:
Didaktische Überlegungen und Beispiele*. 2. erw. Auflage. München: Huber.

Rüschoff, B. (1986): "The 'intelligence' of intelligently programmed adaptive CALL
materials for self-study". *System* 14 (Heft 2), pp. 205-210.

Rüschoff, B./Wolff, D. (1991): "Developing and using interactive audio for foreign
language learning". *CALL Austria* 15, pp. 186-203.

Scott, D. (1991): *Human-Computer Interaction: A Cognitive Ergonomics Approach*.
Chichester: Ellis Horwood.

Seyer, P. (1991): *Understanding Hypertext*. Blueridge Summit, Pen.:
Windcrest/McGraw-Hill.

Sinclair, J. (1991): *Corpus, Concordance, Collocation*. Oxford: OUP.

Stevens, V. (1991): "Concordance-based vocabulary exercises: A viable alternative to
gap-fillers". In: Johns, T./King, P. (ed.): *ELR Journal Vol 4: Classroom
Concordancing*. Birmingham: University of Birmingham, Centre for English
Language Studies, pp. 47-61.

Smith, W.F. (ed.) (1989): *Modern Technology in Foreign Language Education*. Applications and Projects. Lincolnwood (IL): National Textbook Co.

Tribble, C./Jones, G. (1990): *Concordances in the Classroom*. A resource Book for Teachers. Harlow: Longman.

Underwood, J./Underwood, G. (1990): *Computers and Learning*. Oxford: Blackwell.

Upmeyer, A./Günther, A. (1994): "Der Einsatz von Intelligenten Tutoriellen Systemen beim Fernlernen". In: Günther, A. (ed.): *Computerbasiertes Training und Fernlernen*. Berlin: Köster, pp. 53-66.

Vilmi, R. (1996) "The HUT email writing project", *CALL Review*, (IATEFL SIG Newsletter) March Edition: pp. 8-9.

Wolff, D. (1994): "Computers in classroom research". *Computers & Education: An International Journal* 23, pp. 133-142.

Wolff, D. (1994): "Neue Technologien und Fremdsprachendidaktik". In: Beck, U./Sommer, W. (ed.): *Learntec 93: Europäischer Kongreß für Bildungstechnologie und betriebliche Bildung - Tagungsband*. Berlin: Springer, pp. 535-548.

Wolff, D. (1994): "Potenzen und Grenzen neuer Medien: Tagungsbericht der Sektion 11 - Neuere Technologien". In: Hirschfeld, U./Fechner, J./Krumm, H.-J. (ed.): *X. Internationale Deutschlehrertagung Leipzig 2.-7. August 1993: Deutsch als Fremdsprache in einer sich wandelnden Welt*. München: Iudicium Verlag, pp. 225-230.

Wolff, D. (1994): "Neue methodische Ansätze im Fremdsprachenunterricht Ein Überblick". In: Kohn, J./Wolff, D. (ed.): *New Methodologies in Foreign Language Learning and Teaching*. Szombathely: Berzsenyi College, pp. 8-24.

Wolff, D. (1993): "New technologies for foreign language teaching". *Foreign Language Learning and the Use of New Technologies: Proceedings of the LINGUA/DELTA Conference London 1993*. Brussels: Commission of the European Communities, pp. 17-28.

Yazdani, M. (1993): "An artificial intelligence approach to second language teaching". In: Yazdani, M. (ed.): *Multilingual Multi Media: Bridging the Language Barrier with Intelligent Systems*. Oxford: Intellect Books, pp. 198-210.

Yazdani, M. (ed.) (1993): *Multilingual Multi Media: Bridging the Language Barrier with Intelligent Systems*. Oxford: Intellect Books.

About the contributors

Elspeth BROADY teaches French, English and Applied Linguistics at the Language Centre, University of Brighton, where she is also responsible for the MA in Media-Assisted Language Teaching. She has published learning materials in a variety of media, including Video and CD-ROM and writes on the uses of technology and learner autonomy in language learning. Between 1992 and 1995, she worked as an Animator and Project Leader for the Council of Europe Workshop 9 on new technologies in vocationally oriented language learning, leading a Research and Development Group investigating language learning activities supported by a video camera.

Graham DAVIES has been active in the area of language technology for over 20 years. He recently retired from full-time employment at Thames Valley University, where he was Director of the National Centre for Computer Assisted Language Learning (1985-90) and Director of the Language Centre (1990-93). He now works as a free-lance consultant. As well as being partner in a software publishing house, he is also Visiting Professor at Thames Valley University, President of EUROCALL and a member of the European Language Council. In 1991 he set up the East European CALL Centre in Hungary under the EC's TEMPUS programme, and he has worked as a consultant to the EC's LINGUA Bureau and SOCRATES Technical Assistance Office. He has published widely in the field of computer assisted language learning. He participated in Council of Europe Workshop 7B as an animator.

Aagot ELSLANDE teaches French, Norwegian, Social Science and Informatics at Sogn Vocational School, Oslo, Norway. She is also the school's International Secretary. This entails developing the school's international projects, among other things students' work experiences in France and England. She has participated in a Norwegian project on the involvement of female students in information and communication technology, and was involved in one of the Council of Europe Workshop 9 R&D groups - developing hypertexts and investigating the use of hypertexts in the classroom.

Mylène GARRIGUES Docteur en Sciences (Language), is a senior lecturer at the University of Marne-la-Vallée where she teaches computational linguistics and multimedia applications. She has led and developed pilot projects on the use of multimedia in the teaching of French as a foreign language. In the context of her research at the Gaspard Monge Institute she is also involved in developing material for text processing of natural languages (dictionaries and electronic grammars). She was Director of Studies for Council of Europe Workshop 7A held at the Centre International d'Etudes Pédagogiques (Sèvres, France).

Lis KORNUM teaches modern languages at Christianshavns Gymnasium, Copenhagen. She is responsible for several projects on information technology and interactive media for the Danish Ministry of Education and for a Council of Europe project on IT in modern language teaching and learning. She is Project manager of a Lingua project on telecommunication in language teaching and learning, and Vice President of EUROCALL and EUROSESAME. She has published learning materials in CALL and interactive video. She was Director of Studies for Council of Europe Workshop 7B on language learning and the use of modern technologies, and participated in the R&D groups on telematics at Workshop 9.

Bernard MORO teaches English at Lycée Xavier Marmier in Pontarlier, France. He started out as an illustrator and translator in Paris, but gave this up to go back to University and became a teacher in 1980. He is involved in teacher training for both IT and general didactics, especially the use of pictures in language teaching. He has authored software applications for language teaching, as well as various hypermedia applications and general textbooks. He is interested in research on both hypermedia technology and the use of the Internet. He participated in Council of Europe Workshop 9 as an animator, and was involved in one of the R&D groups developing hypertexts.

Yvan ROOSELEER has degrees in both Modern Languages and Computational Linguistics. He works for the largest Flemish educational organisation of Catholic schools as an IT Teacher Trainer. He is at present involved in drafting a recommendation on the use of IT in language learning for the Flemish Education Board, and is a member of the CALL working group within the language teaching department of the University of Leuven. He was involved in one of the R&D groups established at Council of Europe Workshop 7.

Dieter WOLFF is Professor of Applied Psycholinguistics at the Bergische Universität Gesamthochschule in Wuppertal, Germany. His main fields of interest are second language comprehension, language learning and language teaching, new technologies and language learning and curriculum development. He has conducted several research projects on the use of new technologies in foreign language learning, and has published widely in both this field and his other fields of interest. He is editor of "Die Neueren Sprachen", the oldest language teaching journal in Germany. He participated in Workshop 9B as a guest speaker.

Erich ZEHNDER has taught languages and linguistics both in Germany and in the USA at university level. At St Cloud University, Minnesota he was Director of the language laboratory, and in Germany he taught English and German at the University of Mainz and at the Mainz Adult Education Center. As Head of the Foreign Language Department of the Mainz AEC (Volkshochschule) and head of the pedagogical section of the Verband der Volkshochschulen von Rheinland-Pfalz he is involved in teacher training, which is now his major task. He was coordinator of one of the R&D groups established at Council of Europe Workshop 9.